Weekend Walks

in Rhode Island

Gormley Trail

Weekend Walks

in Rhode Island

40 Trails for Hiking, Birding
& Nature Viewing

Fourth Edition

Ken Weber

The Countryman Press
Woodstock, Vermont

An Invitation to the Reader

Over time trails can be rerouted and signs and landmarks altered. If you find that changes have occurred along the walks described in this book, please let us know so that corrections may be made in future editions. The author and publisher also welcome other comments and suggestions. Address all correspondence to:

Editor, *Weekend Walks* Series
The Countryman Press
P.O. Box 748
Woodstock, Vermont 05091

Library of Congress Cataloging-in-Publication Data

Weber, Ken.
    Weekend walks in Rhode Island: 40 trails for hiking, birding & nature viewing / Ken Weber.— 4th ed.
        p.   cm.
    Rev. ed. of: Walks and rambles in Rhode Island. c1999.
    Includes index.
    ISBN 0-88150-614-1
    1. Hiking--Rhode Island—Guidebooks. 2. Rhode Island—Guidebooks. I. Title.
GV199.42.R4W44 2005
917.45'044—dc22   2004061797

Cover design by Dede Cummings Designs
Text design and composition by Chelsea Cloeter
Cover photo © Paul Rezendes
Maps by Moore Creative Designs, © 2005 The Countryman Press

Published by The Countryman Press, P.O. Box 748, Woodstock, Vermont 05091

Distributed by W. W. Norton & Company, Inc., 500 Fifth Avenue, New York, NY 10110

Printed in the United States of America

10 9 8 7

For all those who have worked on Rhode Island's walking places over the years, and for those who appreciate this state's unique qualities

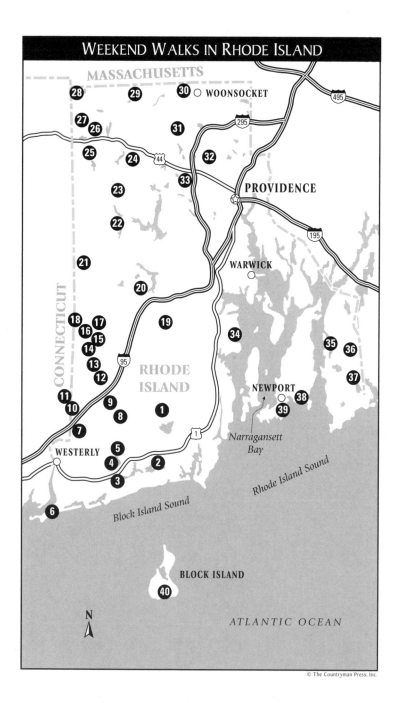

WEEKEND WALKS IN RHODE ISLAND

MASSACHUSETTS

WOONSOCKET

PROVIDENCE

WARWICK

CONNECTICUT

RHODE ISLAND

NEWPORT

WESTERLY

Narragansett Bay

Block Island Sound

Rhode Island Sound

BLOCK ISLAND

N

ATLANTIC OCEAN

© The Countryman Press, Inc.

Contents

Acknowledgments

Sharing trails with amiable companions is the best way to enjoy these walks. I'm indebted to those who accompanied me; they made the walks exceptionally enjoyable. In some cases, my companions brought new perspectives to trails that I've walked dozens of times, and being able to see these places through their eyes made them new and fresh once more. So thank you, to my wife, Bettie; to good friends Joe Healey, Marie Fontaine, Gary Point, Judianne Point, and Jim Gass; to my son, Scott Weber; and to my newest walking buddies, grandchildren Tyler Weber and Abby Weber.

Also, I'm grateful to others who helped significantly, either by joining me for walks in their home areas or by providing information: Ginny Leslie, Garry Plunkett, Jim Spears, Todd McLeish, and Chris Littlefield. This book would have been far more difficult to complete without their assistance.

Introduction

Walking is probably the easiest, safest, cheapest, and most satisfying way to explore an area. Fortunately for those who live in and near Rhode Island, there are a *great* many places to explore in this little state, and there's much to see and experience along the way.

I've been walking Rhode Island trails for more than 30 years now, and I continue finding new places to visit as more property is set aside by the state or individual towns or conservation organizations. And going back to more familiar places is rewarding, too; sometimes we forget just how beautiful a forest or pond or beach is if we haven't been there in a few years.

While many of the trails in this book were detailed in my earlier books—*25 Walks in Rhode Island*, the three editions of *Walks & Rambles in Rhode Island*, and *More Walks & Rambles in Rhode Island*—other trails are described for the first time. Included in that category are such places as Sprague Farm in Glocester, Blackstone Gorge in North Smithfield, Carbuncle Pond–Moosup River in Coventry, Rome Point in North Kingstown, and Browning Mill Pond–Roaring Brook in Exeter. For the past two years I have been walking Rhode Island in trying to decide on the 40 trails to include in this book. I found myself rerouting some of the older trails, to make loop walks, to include features skipped before, to make them easier for families, or simply to to make them more interesting.

The walks are arranged geographically, starting with one of the state's unique places, the Great Swamp, and then going clockwise around the southwestern, western, northern, and eastern areas before featuring another special place, Block Island.

Because all of the walks are loops, they enable you to return to the point where you began without more than slight backtracking. It is important that you read the descriptions before starting out in order to best prepare yourself. The descriptions not only tell you how long the walk is in both miles and time, but how difficult it may be and what you are likely to see along the way. I've also tried to recommend best times of the year for each walk and indicate whether the trails link with other paths and, thereby, can be extended or shortened.

Approximate walking times are subjective; many hikers could do these walks in far less time than listed. But I don't consider walking a competitive sport or endurance event. Those who plunge ahead—never stopping, looking neither left nor right—miss far too much. There is so much beauty, history, and wildlife along these routes it would be a shame not to see as much as possible, and that takes a little slowing down and occasional stops.

Those who would like more detailed maps should obtain U.S. Geological Survey topographic sheets (available at many sporting goods stores). In addition, the Rhode Island Department of Environmental Management prints maps of its management areas, and both The Nature Conservancy and the Audubon Society of Rhode Island can provide maps of their properties that are open to the public.

Putting together this book gave me a good chance to gauge again the status of Rhode Island hiking. Simply having so many trails to choose from in close proximity speaks volumes about the efforts to protect land, to set it aside for public enjoyment. And, as I wrote when preparing *Walks & Rambles in Rhode Island,* I found myself getting excited all over again about the state's walking places. If you haven't been on these paths before, you are in for a treat. If you are walking them again after not having seen them for a few years, I think you will relish the experience. I did.

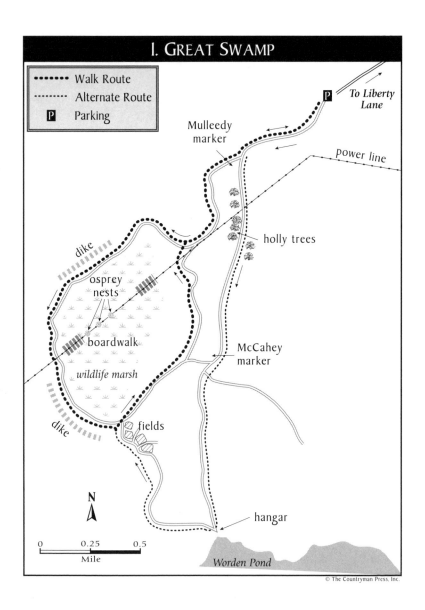

I. GREAT SWAMP

Walk Route
Alternate Route
P Parking

To Liberty Lane

Mulleedy marker

power line

dike

osprey nests

holly trees

boardwalk

wildlife marsh

McCahey marker

fields

N

hangar

0   0.25   0.5
Mile

Worden Pond

© The Countryman Press, Inc.

1 · Great Swamp

Walking distance: 4 miles
Walking time: 2 to 2½ hours

One of the reasons for choosing one walk over another is the chance to see something different. At the Great Swamp in South Kingstown you will see several things not normally found elsewhere, particularly holly trees and ospreys.

The route described here is an easy 4-mile loop that wanders by management fields and follows a dike around an intriguing wildlife marsh that is home to beavers, ospreys, and numerous waterfowl. Those who want a longer walk can add an alternate trail that visits more woodland and an old seaplane hangar at the edge of a large pond.

The 3,400-acre Great Swamp is one of the state management areas that cater to sportspeople, but in doing so it also contributes immensely to the proliferation of wildlife. Once, this area was the last stronghold of Rhode Island's American Indians; now it is home to many plants and animals that have been decimated elsewhere in the state.

The best time to make this walk is spring, when migrating songbirds fill the bushes; ducks, geese, and other waterbirds are nesting in the marsh; and the ospreys are returning to nests atop power-line poles. Bring binoculars and perhaps a camera with a telephoto lens. The lanes are open in other seasons as well, and each time of year has its charm here, but remember that the swamp draws many hunters in late autumn and early winter.

Access

To reach the Great Swamp, take RI 138 to the village of West Kingston, turn west (a sign points the way) onto Liberty Lane, and follow the paved road just under a mile until it ends at a railroad track. Then go left on a gravel lane about 1 mile, passing office and maintenance buildings, and park in an open lot at a barred gateway.

Trail

You will walk on access roads throughout this hike. The woods are both damp and dense, in some areas nearly impenetrable. But there is no need to leave the roads; you can see so much from the flat, open lanes.

Tall trees shade the road at the start, and the understory of young dogwoods, blueberry bushes, blackberries, and pepperbushes adds colorful variety. In spring you are likely to see violets beside the road; in summer there will be pretty purple flowers called deer grass; and in winter the bright red berries of the black alder practically glow against the stark background. Autumn, of course, has the showy foliage. On spring walks you can expect to see and hear catbirds, towhees, orioles, ovenbirds, and numerous species of warblers along this route. When you reach the marsh, waterfowl, ospreys, and swallows take over.

In less than ½ mile the road splits at a marker honoring Dr. John Mulleedy, a late hiking-club leader. (If you want to make the longer walk to Worden Pond and the hangar, take the left fork. It will take you past another granite marker, this one memorializing George McCahey, also a prominent hiker of years past. Taking this fork adds about 1½ miles to the walk and the route from the hangar to the marsh can be a bit confusing. See the map.) For the walk described here, keep to the right at the Mulleedy marker. This road leads more directly to the wildlife marsh, the most interesting feature of the Great Swamp.

After running along an open field, one of many maintained for wildlife, the road reaches and runs along a clearing cut for the power line. In this area you may see bluebirds and other songbirds. Soon, the road forks again. Once more, go right, downhill. In a matter of moments you will reach the dike built in the 1950s to create the 140-acre marsh.

The dike is more than a mile long and many people who come here for the wildlife consider it the best segment of the entire walk. Just as you

Most of the Great Swamp walk is on open lanes.

begin walking on the dike, look to your left. Across the open channel is a beaver lodge, the most visible of several lodges in the marsh. Numerous wood-duck boxes dot the shallow water, and swimming among the water lilies and other aquatic plants are usually ducks, swans, and geese. Herons and kingfishers are common, too, and swallows fill the air (and most of the duck houses).

More likely to capture your attention, however, are the ospreys, the big, fish-eating hawks once close to extinction in Rhode Island. To the left you can see the string of power-line poles across the marsh, and balanced atop many of the poles are the ospreys' bulky nests. No other place in the state has as many ospreys as the Great Swamp, and the grassy dike offers superb views of the graceful birds soaring and sometimes diving into the water.

Along the right side of the curving dike is shallow water that features turtles, frogs, and wildflowers. Chances are you'll find deer tracks on the dike, and once my wife and I saw a beautiful young buck running full speed toward us here. It came within a few yards before veering off.

Take a break when you reach the power line and watch the ospreys. Beyond the power line you'll see a stream off the right side of the dike. This is the Pawcatuck River, flowing out of Worden Pond. Canoeists traveling along the river frequently stop here for a look at the marsh and its inhabitants.

At the end of the dike is a culvert with two large pipes extending into the marsh. This system was installed as a compromise with beavers, which had repeatedly dammed the outlet and raised water levels too high.

Now you are leaving the marsh for a while. The road runs uphill and then makes a sweeping curve to the left, passing some open fields and considerable forest. In the fields are numerous bluebird boxes, which usually attract more swallows than bluebirds. A feature of the forest is the holly tree. These trees, so eagerly sought at Christmastime, are abundant along this road. Look but don't disturb—they are protected by law. The hollies are especially vibrant in early winter, when red berries embellish the shiny green foliage, but they also stand out in early spring, before the surrounding trees and bushes open their leaves.

When you again reach the power-line strip, you can detour on a path to your left for a closer look at the marsh and the osprey nests. The main road swings to the right, re-enters the woods briefly, passing more holly trees, and then rejoins the road you walked earlier. Go to the right and reverse your entrance walk back to the parking lot.

2 · Trustom Pond

Walking distance: 3 miles
Walking time: 1½ to 2 hours

Trustom Pond is for the birds—and that's the way the people who manage the place want it. On this walk, you will see a great variety of birds and will note just how much effort has been put into making this coastal sanctuary appealing to them.

Trustom Pond National Wildlife Refuge encompasses far more than the saltwater pond of its name. The refuge also takes in what once was a farm and the trails run along open fields, through abandoned pastures now being reclaimed by forest, and past low-lying marshes. You can visit each terrain on this 3-mile walk and, as a bonus, see a windmill left over from the days when this was a thriving sheep farm belonging to the Alfred Morse family, which eventually donated the property to the U.S. Fish and Wildlife Service.

Throughout the area, there are birdhouses and nesting aids for birds ranging from ospreys to bluebirds to wood ducks. On a good day, perhaps a sunny morning in May, you might find as many as 40 or 50 species of birds on this easy, comfortable ramble. The large pond is also a stopping place for migrant waterfowl and as such is a popular spot for birders to visit in spring, fall, and even midwinter when the pond is not frozen. To help birders, observation towers have been built at several strategic points, and this refuge has an additional attraction, a handicapped-accessible trail that runs from the parking lot to a small pond and a wooden observation deck.

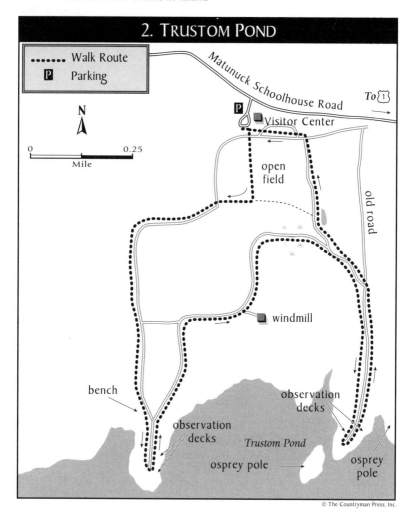

2. TRUSTOM POND

Walk Route
Parking

N

0   0.25
Mile

Matunuck Schoolhouse Road

To 1

Visitor Center

open field

old road

windmill

bench

observation decks

observation decks

Trustom Pond

osprey pole

osprey pole

© The Countryman Press, Inc.

Access

To reach the refuge, take US 1 in South Kingstown to Moonstone Beach Road. Follow that road south 1 mile and turn right on Matunuck Schoolhouse Road. The refuge entrance is 0.7 mile on the left.

Trail

At the parking lot, take a moment to visit a small visitor center, which is staffed by volunteers on most weekends in warm-weather months. Feeders near the building will provide your first look at the refuge birds. The entrance path leads first to a kiosk, which describes the sanctuary and outlines the trails, called the Osprey Point Trail and the Otter Point Trail. On the walk described here, you'll travel both paths.

On the short stroll to the trails' starting points, you pass through a thicket of bushes where you are likely to find warblers, catbirds, towhees, thrashers, and other songbirds. When you emerge into a large field, restored to native big bluestem grass, look for swallows, bluebirds, and maybe a hunting marsh hawk or short-eared owl.

The trail to the left is the path accessible to wheelchairs. It runs to the small Farm Pond, which may have wood ducks and almost always, in warm weather, contains turtles, frogs, dragonflies, and similar pond creatures. That path is part of Otter Point Trail and, unless that pond is your prime objective, will be your return route.

Instead, follow the trail that cuts straight across the large field. This is Osprey Point Trail. It is marked with signs and arrows and is easy to follow. After crossing the field, Osprey Point Trail turns to the right, following a stone wall. (Another trail goes left and connects with the Otter Point Trail near Farm Pond.) The trail to the right soon turns left and runs through an area filled with bushes and small trees. There are a great many wild berries growing here—blueberries, raspberries, wild cherries, viburnums—and consequently birds are usually abundant. Robins, catbirds, jays, orioles, and many, many others congregate here in summer. You're also likely to see deer tracks, or the deer themselves, in this area.

Where the trail meets another path coming in from the left, you will see a wooden bench. You will eventually take this other path, but first follow the main lane south, out onto a point that reaches into Trustom Pond. Usually, there are terns, geese, ducks, and swans on the pond. Two observation decks provide good views to the east, and on that side you

Observation towers help birders at Trustom Pond.

can see a small island on which a pole and platform have been installed for ospreys. The platform nest is often in use and you may want to linger here, watching the graceful fish hawks. At the very tip of the point is the second observation tower, and there is much to see. One birder recently identified 46 species from this tower on a single October day. The sand dune across the pond, Moonstone Beach, is also a bird refuge.

When ready to resume walking, go back up the trail to the fork at the bench. The cutoff, now on your right, is narrow and winding but easy to walk. It runs through another thicket of small trees, including some apples, and follows a stone wall briefly before reaching a grassy lane. Take this lane to the right.

Now you are entering an area used as a sheep pasture shortly before the land became a refuge. The sheep barn formerly stood just to your right, on the opposite side of the stone wall. Now the entire area is quickly reverting to forest. Where the trail makes a turn to the left, look to your right for a view of the windmill, perhaps the last reminder of the sheep, other than the stone walls. The windmill, several yards off the trail, in the shadow of tall trees, no longer pumps water but the blades still spin in the breezes, adding a pleasant touch to the scene.

From the windmill, you'll go through a dense, damp thicket, crossing the wettest area on a wooden walkway, then pass a side trail on the left. You will walk this side path later, but for now, continue straight ahead to an old road that follows a line of trees and still another stone wall. Turn right on this shady, picturesque road and follow it south out to a second point in Trustom Pond.

This point is lovely indeed, with sea breezes, more birds, and more pond views. Once, the Morses' cabin stood here. Now only a pump, a tiny shed, and a few relic apple trees remain from the family retreat.

At the point, benches and an observation tower make the birding easy and comfortable. A second osprey pole stands to the east and the shallow water to the west of the point is a haven for shorebirds as well as larger waterfowl.

When you return up the old road, take the path (now on your left) that you walked earlier, then take the cutoff to the right just before the damp thicket. This trail curls around tiny Farm Pond, which is equipped with a pier, an observation deck, and wood-duck houses. Whether you see wood ducks or not, you are fairly sure to see turtles and frogs.

Beyond the pond, follow the wheelchair-accessible trail as it runs along the large field and then turns left. You'll be passing the refuge maintenance buildings, on your right. This lane will take you to the trailhead and the thicket you walked through when you left the kiosk. Chances are, the warblers and catbirds will still be there, waiting for you.

3 · Ninigret Wildlife Refuge

Walking distance: 3½ miles
Walking time: 2 to 2½ hours

Save this walk for spring or fall. Pick a sunny day when you have time for a leisurely stroll. The rewards can be an abundance of migratory creatures—both birds and butterflies—and you might get such bonuses as a deer or fox sighting. A raised platform also can help you spot waterfowl on a large saltwater pond.

Ninigret National Wildlife Refuge, 400-plus acres, was established on an abandoned naval training site in Charlestown and has undergone considerable improvement in recent years, including removal of most of the old runways and restoration of native grasses. All of the 3½-mile route described here is on marked, easy-to-walk trails, and you can extend your walk on other paths.

Nearby are Ninigret Park, which has numerous attractions including tennis and basketball courts, a bicycle course, a fitness trail, a nature center, and an observatory, and Ninigret Conservation Area, which offers miles of beach walking.

Access

Drive US 1 west of the village of Charlestown and look for the sign for Ninigret National Wildlife Refuge. Access to the trails is also available through Ninigret Park, but for this walk use the refuge entrance on Route 1. To the south of the parking lot is a kiosk; take a moment to look over the information posted there. Trail maps are usually available.

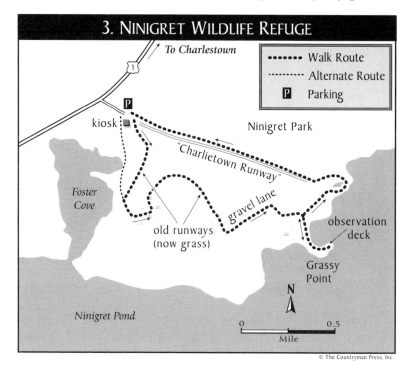

3. NINIGRET WILDLIFE REFUGE

To Charlestown

•••••• Walk Route
·········· Alternate Route
P   Parking

kiosk

Ninigret Park

"Charlietown Runway"

Foster Cove

gravel lane

old runways (now grass)

observation deck

Grassy Point

Ninigret Pond

N

0   0.5
Mile

© The Countryman Press, Inc.

Trail

The trail running in front of the kiosk is called Foster Cove Nature Trail and you could take it for a short loop. For a more extensive look at the refuge, however, connect the various trails. Go south on the nature trail, toward the coast. You are walking parallel to one of the old airstrips now planted in tall bluestem and other grasses.

In less than ½ mile, you reach the Runway Trail; turn left and cross the old runway. This trail quickly goes into a narrow path flanked by small ponds and wetlands. In this area you are likely to see many songbirds and probably footprints of deer, foxes, and other mammals. The path, grassy and flat, crosses one open lane and then emerges at another former runway being restored to native grasses.

Grassy Point's tower offers great views of Ninigret Pond.

Cross this strip, also, then walk a gravel lane to a cutoff, on the right, to the Grassy Point Trail. This is the most popular segment of the refuge because it leads out to Grassy Point itself, an idyllic spot reaching into Ninigret Pond. On the way, you'll pass little wetlands filled with cattails, frogs, and birds. In autumn, migrating monarch butterflies gather along the coast before flying south. Marsh hawks (northern harriers) sometimes hunt here, too, and we once came across a bittern in this area in October.

At a Y-intersection, turn right. The trail then curves along a finger of land between wet areas on its way to Grassy Point. An observation tower at the point enables visitors to get a good look at Ninigret Pond, the largest coastal salt pond in Rhode Island. You are likely to see swans, geese, and ducks of many varieties here, depending on the season. On a spring visit here, my wife and I were treated to the sight of a huge flock of glossy ibises gliding just a few yards above us. In summer, you also are likely to see people fishing or wading in the water in pursuit of clams and crabs.

Across the water, between the pond and the ocean, is a narrow strip of sand and dune grass known as Ninigret Beach. It is also part of the wildlife refuge. Access to the beach is from East Beach Road a few miles west.

When ready to resume your walk, return to the trail junction and take the other leg, now on your right. This path curls around a small pond—turtles, birds, butterflies—and then runs along the edge of Ninigret Pond and provides more good views. Completion of this little loop returns you to a portion of an old airstrip near the refuge's entrance from Ninigret Park.

At this writing, this runway has not been torn up. It is still called Charlietown in recognition of its use by the Charlestown Naval Auxiliary as a landing field. The final segment of your walk is a straight-ahead stroll along the old runway all the way back to your car.

4 · Vin Gormley Trail

Walking distance: 8¼ miles
Walking time: 3½ to 4 hours

This long trail, around Watchaug Pond in Burlingame State Park in Charlestown, is meant for slow, contemplative strolling. It is fairly easy and, while not spectacular, it offers a good variety of attractions, from the large pond itself to damp lowlands to rugged rock ledges to lively little brooks and streams.

Renamed in the 1990s for the late John Vincent "Vin" Gormley, who maintained the trail well into his 80s, the trail also breaks out onto roads at times, which can be either a blessing or a curse, depending on your perspective. It runs through both a quiet wildlife sanctuary and a busy campground, but most of this walk is in forest. The trail is well used, well blazed, and well maintained. Still, while the yellow blazes are easy to follow, some care must be taken because the trail joins and leaves other lanes and paths many times. So don't spend all your time admiring the trees; keep one eye on the yellow marks, particularly the double blazes, which in the Appalachian Mountain Club system indicate changes of direction. You also will be following blue blazes for the long North South Trail for several miles.

There have been several recent improvements to the trail, including a trailhead sign with a map, wooden walkways over muddy areas, mile markers, and, most impressive of all, a covered bridge equipped with benches.

I suggest making this walk in spring or fall. Autumn walks are colorful because of the abundance of hardwood trees, but spring might be even better because seasonal brooks add a flair that includes a couple of minor waterfalls in the second half of the walk.

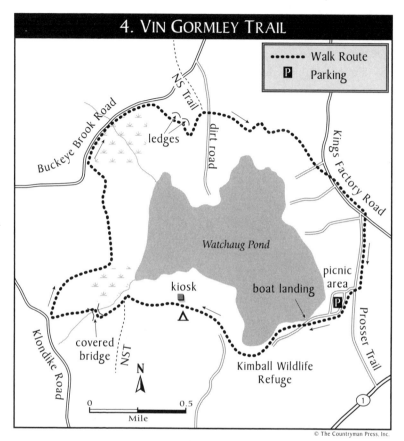

4. VIN GORMLEY TRAIL

······ Walk Route
P Parking

NS Trail

Buckeye Brook Road

ledges

dirt road

Kings Factory Road

Watchaug Pond

kiosk

boat landing

picnic area

P

covered bridge

NST

Klondike Road

Prosser Trail

Kimball Wildlife Refuge

1

N

0   0.5
Mile

© The Countryman Press, Inc.

Access

Except for the section that includes paved roads, the entire trail is within Burlingame State Park and an Audubon Society of Rhode Island wildlife refuge. I think the best starting place is the picnic area on the east shore of Watchaug Pond. Here, there is not only a large parking area but walkers can use the tables for a post-walk lunch and maybe take a swim. The official start, with the trailhead sign, is at the far end of the Burlingame campground, but driving there isn't always easy and access may not be possible in winter. The Watchaug Pond start is considerably better.

Drive RI 1 southbound west of RI 2 and RI 112, following signs for Burlingame Park, until reaching a paved road called Prosser Trail on the right. Follow Prosser 0.6 mile to the park entrance on the left. Immediately, you should see the yellow blazes for the Gormley Trail, which follows this entrance into the park and runs along the outer edge of the parking lot. I suggest leaving your car at the extreme left end of the lot.

Trail

Begin by going left (as you face the pond) from the parking lot onto a road. Almost immediately you pass a mile marker on a tree; it reads Mile 6.5. Since the entire circuit is a little more than 8 miles, this means you are more than 1½ miles from the official start.

The road passes a string of houses and the park's boat ramp before entering the Kimball Wildlife Refuge, the Audubon Society sanctuary that is an old favorite for area birders. Upon entering the refuge, the yellow trail leaves the roadway and breaks off to the right. In this section, the trail runs closer to the 573-acre pond than at any other point in your walk, and you can take side trails to the water's edge. You may see paths blazed in other colors here too—they are part of the Kimball trail system—so be sure to return to the yellow trail if you wander off.

You will be in the refuge only briefly before entering Burlingame Camping Area, the state's largest public campground, about 1 mile from your start. Because the trail cuts directly through the campground, you have to be careful in following blazes. You enter between the camp store, on your left, and a playground area. In summer, this is a bustling little city. At the first paved road, look closely for blazes; they lead you to the right around a traffic island. Then you follow a camp road and cross another traffic island before leaving the campground on a grassy lane, beside the trailhead map and a "Hikers Only" sign between campsites numbered 493 and 494.

Now you are entering dense, damp forest but the trail remains wide and easy to walk. In minutes, the yellow blazes are joined by blue markers because the North South Trail (NST) that goes the length of Rhode

This covered bridge is a great addition to Vin Gormley Trail.

Island comes in from the left. For almost 4 miles you will be following both yellow and blue blazes.

In this segment you begin finding the raised walkways and new bridges that carry hikers over muddy areas that formerly plagued Gormley Trail users. The trail crosses brooks, winds through thick stands of mountain laurel and other bushes, and passes stone walls. The best crossing is provided by the covered bridge over Perry Healy Brook. It is just beyond the Mile 1 marker, meaning you are slightly over 2½ miles into your walk.

As you seem about to emerge on a paved road (Klondike Road), the trail makes a sharp right turn beside a stone wall and remains in forest. This leads to an attractive section that features a mixture of pines and hardwoods accented with boulders and brooks. Next, the trail joins an old lane flanked with delightful trees and stone walls, a stretch particularly inviting in autumn. You follow this lane for about ½ mile, then the yellow-blue trail turns off, to the right. Be sure to make this turn (it is well marked) because staying on the lane would lead you astray.

For the next mile the trail curves around through farmland returned to forest, as evidenced by the many stone walls. Your path joins and leaves other lanes, so you again have to pay attention to the yellow and blue blazes. When the trail emerges on a paved road, you are on Buckeye Brook Road. Take it to the right. You'll pass a swampy area and cross a stream but your stay on the pavement is only ¼ mile before returning to the woods at Mile 3 on the right.

Now you are going downhill into a beech grove that shades the largest ledges along the trail. You walk at the base of jagged glacial rocks, some with cavelike overhangs, and you can take side paths to the tops of several little cliffs. These ledges are a great place to rest and linger a while.

Beyond the ledges, the trail is very curvy as it gradually climbs away from the unseen pond and it is in this area where the blue North South Trail finally leaves the yellow trail, turning left at a T-intersection and going out to Buckeye Brook Road and the Burlingame North Trail (Walk 5). The yellow trail, again labeled "Hikers Only" although tire tracks show other users, crosses a walkway, then reaches a private gravel road at Mile 4. You cross the road and walk through a rocky section laced with brooks. Again, from time to time, you follow old lanes briefly and, at one point, shortly after passing the gravel road, you cross a small brook that, in spring, cascades into a lovely little falls just to the right of your path. Farther ahead, about 6½ miles into your walk, you reach another spot where a spring brook sweeps directly over an outcropping that is part of the trail. This is another good place for a pause, and a bench has been installed here for that purpose. Both of these little waterfalls dry up in summer.

The trail passes an immense, flat table rock (on the left), then crosses another private roadway. Immediately beyond this road, the trail returns to forest behind a house but in minutes you break out of the woods for the final time onto a paved road at Mile 5.5. This is Kings Factory Road. The yellow blazes turn right for the return to Watchaug Pond. Follow Kings Factory Road to the first intersection, then go right on Prosser Trail to the park entrance. Cross the parking lot to your car, or head for the picnic tables beside the pond.

5 · Burlingame North

Walking distance: 4 miles
Walking time: 2½ to 3 hours

This area, the Burlingame Wildlife Management Area, is not nearly as well known as adjoining Burlingame State Park and the Vin Gormley Trail (Walk 4), but it is a gem in its own right. It is a terrific place to walk in all seasons, but especially inviting in spring, when the brooks are running fast and the birds are back to serenade you.

There are no formal hiking trails in this part of the 2,400-acre preserve, but a network of old roads enable visitors to make their own loops. The entry road is blazed in blue because it is part of the North South Trail and the only segment of the recommended route not on open lanes is blazed in white, so there is little chance of losing your way. However, at this writing, trail signs that helped hikers in the past are gone.

Attractions here, in addition to the birdlife and the variety of trees, include two high stone dams left over from an earlier era, an earthen dam and the wildlife marsh it created, many stone walls that wander all over the forest, ledges and rock outcroppings, and, if you make the full 4-mile circuit, a visit to a canoe campground on the banks of the Pawcatuck River.

Since this section of Burlingame is a management area, it is open to hunters in late fall and winter. Anyone using the property at that time must wear fluorescent orange. Spring may be a better time to visit. June is good, too, because then you get the bonus of flowering mountain laurel.

Access

Drive RI 216 in Charlestown to Buckeye Brook Road, turn east, and follow Buckeye Brook Road 1.9 miles to a marked parking area on the north (left) side of the road.

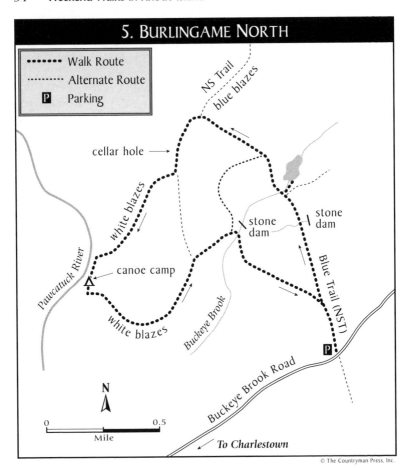

5. BURLINGAME NORTH

······· Walk Route
········ Alternate Route
P Parking

NS Trail
blue blazes

cellar hole →

white blazes

Pawcatuck River

canoe camp

white blazes

stone dam

stone dam

stone dam

Buckeye Brook

Blue Trail (NST)

Buckeye Brook Road

N

0   0.5
Mile

P

← *To Charlestown*

© The Countryman Press, Inc.

Trail

Pines shade the first segment of the entrance road. You will be following the blue blazes of North South Trail, which cross Buckeye Brook Road from Burlingame Park. Here you also will see the first of many outcroppings, on the right, and the first of even more stone walls, also on the right. There is virtually no time on this walk when you are out of sight of stone walls.

At a Y-junction, about ¼ mile from your start, follow the blue North–South Trail (NST) blazes to the right (you will return on the left fork). Now there is more variety in the forest, with hemlocks and many species of hardwoods along the road in addition to pines.

About ½ mile from your start is the first of the old stone dams, on the right. Once, the dam created a pond; now, very little water gathers behind it. At the next junction, however, where a grassy lane branches off to the right, you can see, just ahead and to the right, an earthen dam that is still in use. Take one of the paths to the dike. The impounded marsh water often hosts waterbirds (there are nesting boxes for wood ducks) and otters are seen here occasionally. The stream dammed here is Buckeye Brook, for which the paved road was named. This spot is about ⅔ mile into your walk.

Back on the main trail, you pass several seasonal pools, which in spring may reverberate with the calling of frogs. The lane curves considerably, weaving around the hollows and outcroppings. At about 1¼ miles, you reach another lane going to the left. This one, formerly labeled Ledges Trail, can be used as a shortcut if so desired. Flanked by outcroppings, it curls through the forest and rejoins the main woods road and can be taken back toward the parking area. However, making that choice would mean missing some of the area's highlights.

Instead, stay on the entrance road and follow the blue blazes. However, at the next fork, the blue marks turn right and soon leave state property. Continue following the road as it curves to the left. This is a particularly inviting segment with tall trees, stone walls on both sides, and a wide, easy-to-walk lane. Deer and coyote tracks and signs of wild turkeys are common here, and in spring you may see a few brave blossoms on the remnant apple trees in a long-abandoned orchard on the right. Just beyond this orchard, buried in a tangle of vines and briars, is the cellar hole of a vanished home.

The next point to look for is a gated lane, going to the right, marked with white blazes. Take this detour; it goes to the river and canoe camp. The ⅔-mile walk to the river runs mostly downhill. The grassy lane is

Pause for a while along the Pawcatuck River.

flanked with dense brush that offers excellent birding in spring. The lane emerges in a clearing just above a bend in the wide Pawcatuck, beside the foundation of what was a large building. This is where canoeists pull ashore and camp.

The white-blazed trail runs behind the camping area, but I suggest leaving it for a path along the water's edge. This path, which links the various campsites, offers several good views of the river. In summer, this campground is often filled, particularly on weekends, but in spring it can be a good place to look, listen, and linger.

When ready to resume walking, return to the white-blazed trail. The open lane it was following ends at the campground, but the trail goes on as a footpath. Look for the double blazes that indicate the white trail is turning to the left (east). There are many paths in this area and the white trail can be easy to miss. Narrow at its start, it weaves through the woods, skirting a low, damp area, then gradually makes its way uphill through forest that features huge boulders, stone walls, and immense stands of ferns. This footpath segment, about $3/4$ mile long, emerges on the old woods road that you left earlier to view the river.

Taking the road to the right, you walk beneath towering oaks for about $1/3$ mile until reaching the shortcut trail you passed earlier, now joining from the left. Just steps beyond this junction, you cross Buckeye Brook again. On the left, almost hidden in foliage in summer, is the second high stone dam, and it is worth inspecting. Reinforced and reshaped with cement in the 1940s, the open gate forms a picturesque waterfall when the brook is running high. It is another pretty spot where lingering is easy.

From the dam, the road runs just about $1/2$ mile, beneath surging forest and beside stone walls, before ending at the blue-marked entrance road. Turn right for the return to your car.

6 · Napatree Point

Walking distance: 3 miles
Walking time: 2 to 2½ hours

Save this walk for autumn or winter, when the swimmers and sun-bathers have gone, the tourists have departed, and the boating activity around the nearby Watch Hill Yacht Club has diminished—or maybe early spring. Then, Napatree Point is a great place to walk.

Napatree Beach is as far west as you can go in Rhode Island and farther south than any other mainland point. It reaches out into Little Narragansett Bay below Westerly like a slim, J-shaped finger.

All barrier beaches are fragile and Napatree is one of the most fragile. Once it extended much farther into the sea, but the hurricane of 1938 broke through it. The devastation was immense, with several lives lost and practically all the houses and cottages that then lined the beach destroyed. Now there are no buildings on the point, only the remains of a military fort, and the narrow strip of land is literally held in place against the forces of the sea by its vegetation. For that reason, take extra care not to walk on or disturb the plants and bushes growing down the center of the point.

Napatree Point can be a good place for seeing birds, particularly migrating hawks in fall, but the birds that nest here require consideration from walkers. As a sign indicates, this is an osprey nesting area and sometimes sections of the beach are roped off for the ground-nesting piping plovers. Because of the birds, it is best to leave your dogs at home if you visit in spring or summer.

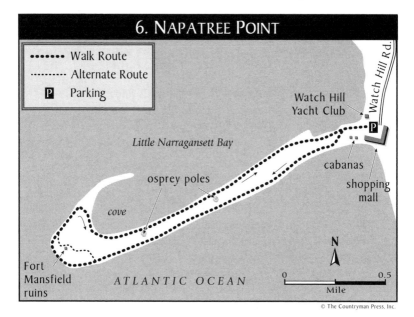

6. NAPATREE POINT

•••••• Walk Route
---------- Alternate Route
P Parking

Little Narragansett Bay

Watch Hill Yacht Club

Watch Hill Rd.

P

cabanas

shopping mall

osprey poles

cove

N

Fort Mansfield ruins

ATLANTIC OCEAN

0   0.5
Mile

© The Countryman Press, Inc.

Access

To reach Napatree Point, take RI 1A to the village of Avondale, then follow Watch Hill Road until it reaches a little shopping center at the water's edge. You can see the yacht club on the right. Finding a parking place in summer is difficult, but at other times of the year you should be able to park along the street or in the mall lot.

Walk through the shopping center parking area and follow a road that runs to the right, past private cabanas, to a fence barrier. There is room at the right end of the wire fence for you to enter the finger of land called Napatree.

Trail

You immediately have a choice. A trail runs along the harbor shore at the right and another goes left over the ridge, between snow fences, toward the sea. For this walk, take the left path, even though walking in the soft sand is tedious. In a few moments you are facing the ocean and walking near the water, where the sand is firmer and less tiring.

Follow the beach southwest. This is the area most crowded in summer, but the entire beach is often deserted in winter, except for a few strollers and an occasional jogger. During September and October, you are likely to find a number of birders in this area, for Napatree is a key spot in the migratory flyway of hawks. When conditions are right, hundreds of hawks of half a dozen varieties will pass over the point in a single day. Migrating shorebirds and songbirds also pass this spot in both spring and fall, but many fly at night, so they are less visible.

Almost immediately you can see, ahead of you, high poles on the dune. They are topped by platforms and have from time to time been used for osprey nests. Ospreys are the big, fish-eating hawks that once were nearly decimated by pesticides. Now they are recovering in numbers and watching the graceful birds as they circle in the sky or dive after fish is a treat for Napatree walkers. Please do not disturb the birds or go too near the nests.

For more than a mile, you can walk a curving shoreline, with gulls and other seabirds riding the waves on your left, sea stars and bits of shells on the beach at your feet, and the low ridge with its beach peas, dusty millers, and other bushes and grasses on your right.

When you finally reach a jumble of large rocks in the water near the point's end, look for a narrow sand path uphill into a thicket of blackberries, bittersweet, and other bushes on the ridge. *Be careful; there is plenty of poison ivy in this thicket.* Hidden there is something most summertime visitors to Napatree know nothing about: the remains of Fort Mansfield. The fort was built around 1900 but almost immediately was found to be indefensible and soon was abandoned and eventually dismantled. All that remains now are a few graffiti-marred low walls and concrete steps, a room or two, and the circular holes for the gun turrets, all hidden from shoreline view by the vines and bushes.

From the fort, however, you have a good view of the osprey nest poles and this also is an excellent place to watch the hawks in fall or to find

Napatree Point provides miles of beach walking.

the songbirds that dally here during migration. The rocky shoreline at the point often turns up sandpipers and other shorebirds, including the striking oystercatchers, black and white birds with bright orange beaks. There often are loons, geese, brant, or cormorants just offshore.

From the fort, you can take paths down to the shore for the return walk along the harbor side. Often there are more birds here than anywhere else along the beach. If you're in no hurry, follow the narrow strip to its end, then return along the edge of the smooth cove that lies inside the curl of the J. Otherwise, you can cross over on one of several paths to the cove and shorten your walk a bit. The cove is interesting because its shallow, calm water offers refuge for ducks and mergansers and also for the many clams, crabs, jellyfish, and other forms of marine life you may see as you walk along.

The return walk along the harbor takes you closer to the osprey poles than you were while walking the ocean side. Footing on the cove shore isn't as smooth as on the sea side—more pebbles than sand—but it's still an easy walk back toward Watch Hill.

The harbor is a very busy place in summer, with boats of all sizes and descriptions coming and going or moored, and boating enthusiasts may want to linger here just as birders often are reluctant to leave the point. By autumn, the boating activity declines dramatically but there are usually some crafts moored in the shallow harbor, except in winter, and the scene draws many photographers and artists.

The entire walk can be done in a couple of hours, but if you like seascapes, migratory birds, boats, and invigorating salt air, it could, and should, take much longer.

7 · Black Farm

Walking distance: 1¾ miles
Walking time: 1 to 1½ hours

Black Farm, one of the state's newer wildlife management areas, is a place to come to for slow, contemplative walking. Rather than spectacular, the 245-acre property is quietly beautiful, with lush groves of pines, lanes carpeted in pine needles, and an idyllic pond. You'll get views of a river and small open fields and, if you wish, walk a section of a long-abandoned railroad bed.

And there is more. On this walk you will cross a hurrying brook in two places, investigate a unique stone structure, and pause at the grave of a Civil War casualty, a soldier who died at the age of 16.

As a management area, Black Farm is open to hunting, so it is best to hike in other seasons than late fall and early winter. Also, be aware that these trails are not blazed, so some care must be taken not to wander off onto other paths.

Access

Black Farm is in Hopkinton, on the Rockville–Alton Road. Take I-95 to Exit 2, and go south. The parking lot is 1½ miles on the left.

Trail

The parking lot is at the end of an open field, so before walking, take a moment to look over the field, which sometimes attracts birds and often features wildflowers. The trail begins at the far right corner of the parking area.

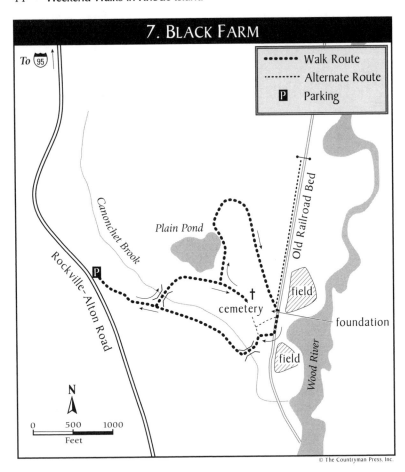

7. BLACK FARM

To 95

••••••• Walk Route
-------- Alternate Route
P Parking

Canonchet Brook

Plain Pond

Old Railroad Bed

Rockville–Alton Road

P

cemetery †

field

foundation

field

Wood River

N

0   500   1000
Feet

© The Countryman Press, Inc.

You begin by walking through mixed woods with what appears to be
a deep hollow on your left. In less than ¼ mile, the trail splits. Take the
left fork; you'll return on the other path.

The left fork drops down a slope and crosses a quick little stream called
Canonchet Brook. At present (2004), the footbridge is prone to being dis-
lodged by spring freshets. A short distance to the left of the bridge, a jumble of rocks shows traces of an old dam, once the site of a mill. Soon

after crossing the bridge, you cross the narrow millrace from the vanished mill, then climb out of the little valley.

The uphill path emerges on an open woods lane near the pond. Turn right (going left leads you to a maze of trails but won't get you to the features of this walk). In moments you reach an open area beside the pond, a good place to drink in the scenery. This is a kettle pond, scoured out by the glaciers thousands of years ago. It has no brooks running in or out of it. Surrounded by towering trees, it resembles some miniature northern mountain lake far more picturesque than its mundane name, Plain Pond.

About 75 yards beyond the pond, you reach an intersection. I recommend turning left—but not yet. First, continue straight ahead for another 100 yards or so, until you see a stone-walled cemetery just off the lane on the left. This family graveyard includes the tombstone of Charles L. Collins, the teenaged Civil War soldier who died on the Mississippi River in 1863. The Collins family once owned this land and his parents are buried beside him. The boy's stone includes this inscription:

> *Dear friends, my country called and I must go,*
> *with leaden wings to face the foe*
> *And should I die on southern shore,*
> *I hope we'll need to part no more.*

When ready to resume walking, return up the lane to the intersection you passed earlier. (Continuing downhill from the graveyard would take you to the old railroad bed, but you would miss some good scenes of the pond and the forest.) Walking the alternate lane, now on your right, takes you close to the pond again and then the trail curls through pine groves so quiet you can almost hear a needle drop.

When you emerge on the open roadway that once was a railroad track, look in the woods just to your right. There you will find a high stone structure that might have been a barn foundation or perhaps a holding pen. What makes it unusual is that some of the corners are the standard 90

Some foundations at Black Farm defy explanation.

degrees and others are rounded, and there are wide openings or doorways on all four sides. There also is a second room, and most of the stones are large rectangular pieces obviously cut with considerable effort. What was this place? I have never found any other stonework quite like it.

At the old railroad bed—now a straight lane—you have a choice. Going to the left is tempting, because the lane resembles a tunnel with the dense pines meeting overhead. Exploring that way is pleasant enough, but before long you will be walking behind houses, and eventually the lane runs off state property and you will have to retrace your steps.

If you turn to the right at the stone foundation, you will be walking along a narrow open field, now on your left, and to the left of the field is the Wood River, perhaps Rhode Island's finest wildlife and canoeing river. In this area, the river is wide and marshy and often attracts ducks, geese, herons, and other birds. Trees line the river but paths provide viewing points.

Beyond the field, the former railroad bed runs through a thin strip of trees, then enters a larger open field where you may see hawks, songbirds, or, if you are very lucky, deer or a fox. At the far end of this field, you should see a lane entering from the right. Take it. Immediately, you see still another junction. The trail to the right would take you back to the cemetery. Instead, take the left fork over a bridge. Unlike the footbridge you crossed earlier, this is a wide, solid bridge. Here, Canonchet Brook is considerably larger than at the old mill site but usually far more sedate.

Just beyond the bridge, you reach another open field. Signs show this area as private property but there is a strip of state land along the lower (to the right of the bridge) edge of the field. Go 50 feet or so into the field and you will find a narrow path running to the right. It will take you across the rest of the field and return you to the woods through an opening in a stone wall.

This trail runs through an attractive section of mixed woods accented by boulders. After passing through gaps at the meeting of two more stone walls, the trail forks. The wider (but older) path goes right, downhill. That was once the lane down to the mill; now it dwindles to almost no path at all. Instead, take the left fork. It carries you back to the parking lot in a matter of minutes.

8 · Carolina South

Walking distance: 3½ miles
Walking time: 2 hours

If you like solitude—a place where you can walk for miles among the trees and brooks and fields without meeting other people—then Carolina South might be ideal (as long as you don't go during hunting season).

This is a walk through the southern section of the 2,200-acre Carolina Wildlife Management Area in Richmond. This route, without detours, is 3½ miles and can easily be done in a couple of hours. It cuts through the interior of the property, past numerous little fields planted for wildlife, then returns on a blazed trail that is part of the North South Trail. However, detours and exploration off the trail can and should be integral to most woodland walks.

Wildlife is likely to be a big part of this walk. The various habitats of Carolina offer chances of seeing deer, wild turkeys, woodcocks, and numerous songbirds. Leaving the trail and examining some of the fields often pays off in bird sightings. There are other attractions, too. At your start is a tiny graveyard and much later you'll pass another cemetery, this one far back in the woods but surrounded by a white picket fence. There also are a couple of cellar holes along the trail, you can linger at a small campsite for canoeists on the Pawcatuck River, and a short detour takes you to an impressive old stone bridge.

Be aware, however, that this area teems with hunters in late fall and early winter and again for a brief period in spring when the wild turkeys are legal game. At most other times, Carolina South is left to the walkers and the wild creatures.

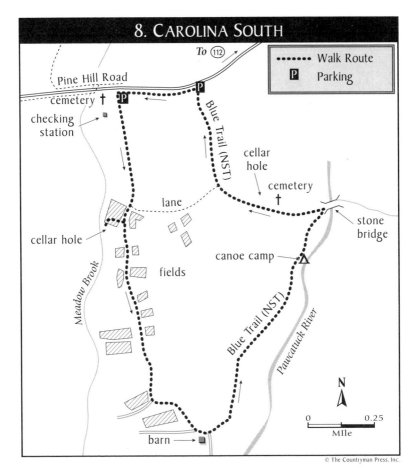

8. CAROLINA SOUTH

Legend:
- ●●●●● Walk Route
- **P** Parking

Map labels: To (112), Pine Hill Road, cemetery †, checking station, Blue Trail (NST), cellar hole, cemetery †, stone bridge, lane, cellar hole, canoe camp, Meadow Brook, fields, Blue Trail (NST), Paucatuck River, N, barn, 0 0.25 Mile

© The Countryman Press, Inc.

The ambitious can easily lengthen their hike by adding the Carolina North loop (Walk 9).

Access

To reach the starting point from the northern part of the state, take RI 138 east (Exit 3 off I-95) to RI 112 just east of Hope Valley. Go south on RI 112 2.5 miles to Pine Hill Road, turn west (right), and proceed for 1.5 miles. On the left is a red hunter checking station with a parking area in front.

Grain fields help attract wildlife at Carolina.

If coming from the coastal area on RI 112, go left on Pine Hill Road just north of the village of Carolina.

Trail

From the parking area, first go a few steps and look over a tiny cemetery in front of the building, near the road. Dates on these stones indicate the last burial was well over a hundred years ago. This grassy little graveyard is a peaceful spot indeed and sets the mood for this walk.

From the checking station you can see the first of many fields planted in grain for wildlife. Take a minute for a look. Often small birds are in this field and I've seen turkeys here. When ready to begin walking, take the lane that runs to the left from the building. This lane will be your trail for the first 1¼ miles of this walk.

The lane begins by running between tall pines, and you might feel you are on a forest walk, but after about ½ mile you return to fields. Most are narrow strips, some are lying along the lane, others are carved out of woods and connected to the lane by short roadways. Don't rush by these fields; you never know when a deer or fox might be feeding right out in the open. Turkeys, coyotes, rabbits, and hawks are other possibilities.

At the far end of the *first* field on your right (after emerging from the woods), you can take a detour for another feature. A path going into the woods at the far corner of this field (see map) leads to a tumbledown cellar hole with a huge foundation for a center chimney. The path is narrow and in summer the cellar might be difficult to find because of sprawling bushes. An even more obscure path continues beyond the cellar to more stonework of the vanished farm and then to a rocky crossing over a stream called Meadow Brook. Exploring this area is not easy but it's fun.

Back on the main lane, you resume alternating between woods and fields. The lane itself often shows deer tracks and in the right seasons you are likely to find many songbirds, butterflies, bees, and other interesting creatures as well.

When the lane reaches a T-intersection, with tall pines ahead, go left. In a few yards, this lane turns to the right and enters a field. Now look to your left; across an open field you can see a dilapidated barn. Follow a narrow path along the left edge of this large field (which is off state property), following the border of the field as it curves toward the barn. On your left will be trees and a low, damp area. The path crosses a grassy area in front of the barn, and just beyond the barn you will see the first rectangular markers for the North South Trail. The trail, going south, crosses the big field near the barn. You, however, are going north, so continue following the edge of the field and the blazes for another 150 yards or so, until they turn to the left into the woods. You can remain with the rectangular markers and the NST's blue blazes for the rest of this walk, although my route includes a couple of short detours.

This trail, an old woods road, is the ultimate in solitude. Carpeted with pine needles, it can be walked in virtual silence. Less than $\frac{1}{2}$ mile after entering this forest, and slightly more than 2 miles from your start, you will reach an unmarked path going to the right. In summer, it can be easy to miss. This short path goes to the canoe camp on the bank of the Pawcatuck River. Years ago, there were outhouses here and more permanent cooking facilities; now it is just a small clearing with enough room for a fire ring and a few small tents. Still, it is a good place to linger, look over the river, and perhaps have lunch.

Back on the trail, you will begin to see large boulders, along with some stone walls, just before the old road forks. The blue blazes go left, uphill. I prefer going straight ahead, downhill, to an ancient stone bridge that crosses one of the brooks that feed the river. The property beyond the bridge is posted, so you will have to turn back here, but the bridge, made of large stone slabs, is worth a look.

Returning to the blue trail is simply a matter of taking the first trail just up from the bridge. It quickly joins the main trail. Just ahead now, on the right, is the second cemetery. This one, guarded by the picket fence, is not as old as the graveyard along Pine Hill Road; some stones are dated after 1900. The fence makes it unusual; most similar graveyards this far back in the woods are surrounded by stone walls.

About ¼ mile beyond the graveyard you should find many stone walls and, just to the right of the trail, an extremely small cellar hole. On the left is a little clearing that formerly included several old apple and pear trees; now there are fewer each year. In time, only the stones will show that people once lived here.

Where the trail forks, almost 3 miles from your start, you have a decision to make. The blue trail goes ahead and the left fork angles back toward the fields area you walked earlier. I usually have difficulty with this decision; the fields present more chances to see wildlife but the blue trail is a delightful stroll beneath towering pines. Consider it a win-win situation.

By staying on the blue trail you will reach a parking area, then Pine Hill Road. Turn left, with the blue blazes, and in ⅓ mile you are back to your car.

9 · Carolina North

Walking distance: $4\frac{1}{2}$ miles
Walking time: 2 to $2\frac{1}{2}$ hours

Save this walk for some bright morning in April, May, or maybe early autumn. At those times, a stroll through the northern segment of the Carolina Wildlife Management Area in Richmond is most rewarding.

In spring, wildlife activity is usually at its best. Carolina was one of the places where wild turkeys were released during a state stocking program in the 1980s and they continue to thrive here. Hearing their gobbling on spring mornings is delightful. Other birds sing in spring, too, and the area's mountain laurel blooms profusely at that time. Autumn's highlights include colorful foliage and invigorating weather.

Be aware, of course, that Rhode Island now has a spring hunting season for turkeys, usually in May, and this area draws many hunters in fall and early winter. As with all state management areas, fluorescent orange must be worn by all visitors from early October until the end of February. Dogs must be leashed between April 1 and August 1.

This $4\frac{1}{2}$-mile walk is called Carolina North because it lies on the north side of Pine Hill Road, which slices through the 2,200-acre management area. There is another ramble called Carolina South (see Walk 8) on the opposite side of Pine Hill Road.

Most of Carolina North's walk is on old management roads. In the past, these roads were labeled with name posts, making the route easy to describe. Now, however, most of those old posts are gone, so finding your way around can be a little confusing. For that reason, I suggest making a loop that runs entirely on the North South Trail (NST) and carries the NST markers and blue blazes.

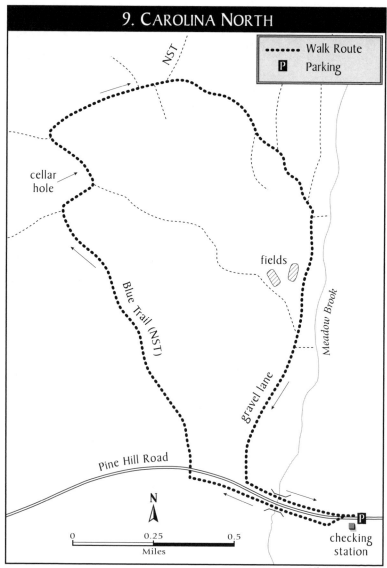

9. CAROLINA NORTH

••••• Walk Route
P Parking

NST

cellar hole

Blue Trail (NST)

fields

Meadow Brook

gravel lane

Pine Hill Road

N

0   0.25   0.5
Miles

P
checking station

© The Countryman Press, Inc.

Access

To reach the starting point for both Carolina walks from the northern part of the state, take RI 138 east (Exit 3 off I-95) to RI 112 just east of Hope Valley. Go south on RI 112 2.5 miles to Pine Hill Road, turn west (right), and proceed for 1.5 miles. On the left is a red hunter checking station with ample parking near the road. If coming from the coastal area, go left on Pine Hill Road just north of the hamlet of Carolina.

Trail

From the checking station, walk Pine Hill Road west, following the blue blazes, and cross a stream called Meadow Brook. At a gravel lane just beyond the bridge you will see NST markers, indicating the trail goes to the right into the forest. This lane is the route designated for horseback riders and bicyclists using the NST. You could turn here but I recommend anybody not familiar with the area continue walking Pine Hill Road a short distance to a hikers-only trail. The NST is poorly blazed in some segments, and for much of the way it is blazed only in one direction. Doing the more difficult stretches *with* the blazes is preferable to repeatedly looking on the far side of trees for blue paint. You will return on the open gravel lane.

The entrance to the hikers-only trail, through a fence with a narrow opening, is opposite utility pole 71 along the paved road. In the early going there are many stone walls and the trail is crowded with young pines. Soon, though, the trail opens considerably and you are walking through a delightful area with tall trees and pockets of mountain laurel. Boulders dot the forest floor, mostly on the right.

After about 1 mile from the paved road you reach a junction. Go right. A stone wall runs along the left side of this road, which is open and easy to walk. You will quickly reach another junction. Be careful here: the main road appears to go right, but you should turn left. There are no blazes at this corner.

The left lane curls left, then right, going slightly downhill. This is a lovely segment with numerous stone walls, a cellar hole on the left, and old apple

Tall trees and open lanes are Carolina features.

trees that continue to blossom in spring. Once, this was somebody's home.

The next junction, just under 2 miles from your start, is blazed better; your trail goes to the right. A turn to the left here would take you to the Carolina Trout Pond, a popular fishing spot. Just after making the turn to the right, look in the woods on the left for considerable stonework that includes fences, perhaps pens for livestock of the vanished farmers.

The road, flanked by thriving ferns, goes uphill for about ⅓ mile to the next junction. Now you turn right onto a narrower lane that runs mostly downhill. You will be passing through mixed woods, including numerous beech trees. At one point, a huge old beech leans over the trail from the right. This tree's trunk is covered with carved initials and dates, some more than 60 years old and some very recent.

Care must again be taken at the next road junction because of poor blazing. The wider trail goes right, the path you should take goes left. (Going right would not be a big error; that path also goes to the open gravel road, but it could cause confusion because you would not find NST blazes, and it would mean missing some interesting features of the suggested walk.)

The trail to the left is short. After going through an area in which stone walls seem to run at haphazard angles, you reach still another junction. This is the spot where the hikers-only trail and the equestrian-bicyclist trail converge. The NST turns to the left from your path and soon leaves state property.

You, however, want to return to Pine Hill Road, so you turn right at this corner and follow the NST markers. Some now show an S for south. The trail is fairly narrow here and several high stone ledges appear in the woods. When you cross a small stone bridge, pause for a few minutes. Beneath the bridge ran a sluice for a mill. Some of the stonework for the mill remains just to the left of your path. Envisioning the effort it took to build the mill in this rocky ground, and the activity that once took place here, adds much to your walk.

This path emerges at the end of the gravel lane you passed earlier. Turn right on the lane for your return to Pine Hill Road. You will pass, on your right, several small fields that are usually planted with grains for wildlife, and a gated lane. Then you will see a lane running to the left. This lane provides access to Meadow Brook. A detour for a look at the stream is short and usually worth the effort.

From this lane it is about $\frac{1}{2}$ mile to the paved road. Most of the way you are walking beneath towering pines and listening to birds. When you reach the paved road, turn left for the short return to your car.

10 · Long Pond–Ell Pond

Walking distance: 5½ miles
Walking time: 3 to 3½ hours

This walk in Hopkinton is through a rocky forest now called the Long Pond–Ell Pond Natural Area, and outstanding natural features are just what you will find. The first section is so spectacular it might be called the "magnificent mile."

In addition to Long Pond and Ell Pond, both of which you will see from high above, you'll visit a bizarre network of stone walls and rock piles near picturesque Ashville Pond, then return via two roads and a retracing of the wonderful segment around Ell Pond and Long Pond. A full circuit is about 5½ miles and will take 3 hours or longer.

Keep in mind, however, that this is not a walk for young children or the out-of-shape. Even though the high bluffs above the pond are barely ¼ mile from your start, you are likely to be huffing and puffing by the time you get there, and the climbs get tougher on the far side of the ponds. With two parking lots available, hikers concerned about the effort required can leave cars at each end of this first segment and do a one-way walk that would include all of the magnificent mile (but not the loop to Ashville Pond). The distance between the parking areas is about 1½ miles.

The yellow-blazed trail is the southern terminus of the Appalachian Mountain Club's (AMC's) Narragansett Trail (Walk 11) that also extends into Connecticut. Included in the full circuit here are the detours to overlooks above ponds, a descent through a rock cleft, pauses beneath towering rhododendrons and hemlocks, a climb over massive outcroppings, and the "bonus" walk to Ashville Pond and back.

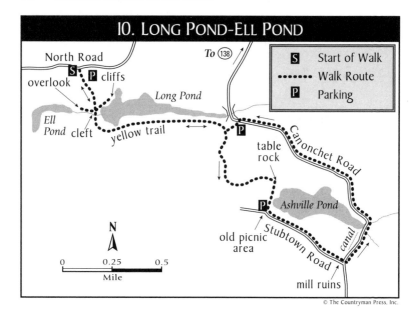

© The Countryman Press, Inc.

In 1974 this area, ownership of which is shared by the state, the Audubon Society of Rhode Island, and The Nature Conservancy, was entered in the National Registry of Natural Landmarks because the site "possesses exceptional value as an illustration of the nation's natural heritage and contributes to a better understanding of man's environment." A plaque with those words is embedded in a boulder above Ell Pond.

The area is spectacular in all seasons, but the abundance of mountain laurel and rhododendron make a visit in early summer extra colorful.

Access

To reach the start of this walk, follow RI 138 to the village of Rockville, near the Connecticut line, turn left onto Wincheck Pond Road, then left (south) onto Canonchet Road. Drive 0.5 mile to North Road (the first right) and follow North 1 mile. After the first 0.5 mile the roadway becomes gravel. Park on the left, where you see a sign and the yellow AMC trail blazes. There is another parking lot 0.5 mile south on Canonchet Road, but the North Road access is closer to the region's best sights.

For a one-way walk, you can leave a second vehicle at Canonchet Road and have a walk of about 1½ miles. Or you can place your second car at a lot on Stubtown Road, near Ashville Pond, and walk about 2½ miles. To reach that lot, follow Canonchet Road about 1½ miles from North Road, turn right onto Stubtown Road, and go just beyond the pond to a small parking lot on the right.

Trail

From the North Road parking area, almost immediately you will be scrambling up, down, and around boulders, but you are just as likely to be looking above your head as under your feet. Some of the tallest wild rhododendrons in the state shade the trail, as do hemlocks and mountain laurel. In early summer the profusion of blossoms creates a gardenlike atmosphere.

After struggling up a huge, angular rock mass, you will reach a sign pointing the way to Ell Pond (right), Long Pond (left), and a hemlock forest (straight ahead, down through the cleft). Explore the side trails; they are worth the time and effort. These side paths are not blazed but are easy to follow.

The Ell Pond path is short, ending atop an outcropping just 30 or 40 yards off the yellow trail, beside the Natural Landmark plaque. Spread out below is narrow, L-shaped Ell Pond, one of Rhode Island's few true bogs. Unfortunately, the view is not as expansive as in years past because of the maturing forest, but it remains a beautiful spot.

No trees obscure the views of Long Pond available by taking a side path off the opposite side of the yellow trail. It's a slightly longer walk but you can climb to bulging cliffs that tower above the pond. This spot is so scenic I always pause here before or after doing the rest of the hike.

Back on the yellow trail, ease yourself down into the cleft. It is steep but an AMC work crew several years ago made the going much easier by

Linger along the outcroppings above Long Pond.

rearranging some of the rocks into something resembling a curving stairway. Solid walls of stone loom above you on both sides.

At the bottom of the cleft, the trail curls to the right and crosses a brook that links the two ponds. The trail then begins climbing again, going left. For the next ½ mile or so, the trail weaves up and around immense boulders and rock masses. The up-and-down scrambling continues until you see a tumbledown stone wall on your right. Now you are nearing the end of the magnificent mile. The trail follows the old wall for several hundred yards atop a stony ridge that provides views (when leaves are down) of the narrowing pond below and a few houses on the opposite shore. When you finally turn to the right, away from the pond, you will be near a short side trail (to the left) that runs to the Canonchet Road parking lot.

At this junction, the yellow blazes make an abrupt turn to the right, going directly into a thicket of mountain laurel. It is slightly more than 1 mile from the Canonchet Road parking lot to Ashville Pond, and it's a far easier walk than the first segment, but nearly as interesting in another manner. If you visit when the laurel is in bloom, you will enjoy this section thoroughly. Then, after leaving the laurel thickets for a more open forest of hardwoods, you'll see the numerous stone walls and rock piles. The walls seem to have been built randomly, running at many angles and directions, and the piles similarly defy explanation. They might have been an effort to make more land available for plowing, but there are so many rocks and huge boulders still scattered about that this would have been an all-but-hopeless cause.

When the trail reaches an immense table rock, you are near Ashville Pond. Here, the trail turns right, then curls down to the water's edge, and soon runs into an old picnic area beside the lovely pond. The trail officially ends at a small parking lot along Stubtown Road.

To return to the starting point, I prefer walking Stubtown Road to the left about ½ mile to Canonchet Road. At this corner, you can see the remains of a mill across from a house that a plaque says was built in 1762. As you take Canonchet Road to the left, you will follow a canal that was built to carry water from Ashville Pond to the mill. The road is built on what was the pond's dam, and on the opposite side of the road you can see the stonework that channeled a brook into the pond.

For the 1 mile from Stubtown Road to the parking lot on Canonchet Road, you walk between two forests. This not a heavily traveled road and walking it can be most pleasant, starting with excellent views of Ashville Pond. On the way, you will pass, on your right, two lanes that run to an unseen state-owned lake called Blue Pond.

When you reach the Canonchet Road parking lot, now on your left, you can pick up the yellow blazes once more. You will be retracing your route over the ridges and cliffs of Long and Ell Ponds, but it's a chance to get another perspective of the magnificent mile.

II · Narragansett Trail

Walking distance: 4½ miles
Walking time: 2½ to 3 hours

This section of the Narragansett Trail is almost entirely in Connecticut, but because the loop begins and ends at the state line, and because it packs so many outstanding features into such a pleasant package, many Rhode Island hikers have adopted it as one of their own. Or, at least, they wish it were one of theirs.

Part of the Appalachian Mountain Club's network of trails, the Narragansett, after crossing the state line into Rhode Island, continues around Yawgoog Pond and then to the Long Pond–Ell Pond region (see Walk 10). This walk also links with the long Tippecansett Trail that runs all the way up to the Arcadia Wildlife Management Area. So, if desired, walkers could begin here and continue north all the way to the Pachaug Trail (Walk 18) and even beyond.

However, for most of us, there is enough to explore and examine just in this loop to make a thoroughly enjoyable day hike. The distance can be as short as 4 miles or as long as 5½, if a circuit of Green Falls Pond is included. Those who simply follow the blazed trail and take no detours, however, may miss some of the special treats of this walk, so I recommend going slowly and exploring some of the massive rock outcroppings just off the trail. There are many such ledges and ridges. Other features include the thickets of mountain laurel, several tumbling brooks, a lovely marsh (not on trail itself), the remains of a spool mill, a log shelter, the picturesque Green Falls Pond, and a magnificent ravine. My listed walk of 4½ miles takes in all of these sights, along with a 1-mile return on a little-used gravel road.

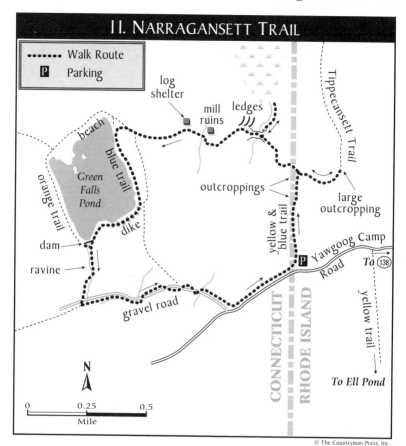

II. NARRAGANSETT TRAIL

••••••• Walk Route
🅿 Parking

log shelter

mill ruins

ledges

Tippecansett Trail

beach

blue trail

orange trail

Green Falls Pond

outcroppings

large outcropping

dike

dam

ravine

yellow & blue trail

🅿 Yawgoog Camp

Road

To 138

gravel road

CONNECTICUT

RHODE ISLAND

yellow trail

To Ell Pond

N

0   0.25   0.5
Mile

© The Countryman Press, Inc.

This is a fairly strenuous walk, with considerable climbing up and down outcroppings. In spring and after heavy rains, you also may have to hop over some of the brooks. Of course, that is when the brooks are most appealing.

Access

To reach the start, drive RI 138 west of the Hopkinton village of Rockville a short distance to Yawgoog Camp Road. Follow the paved road to the entrance of the Yawgoog Scout Camp, then turn right onto the gravel road that runs parallel to the front of the camp. Take the gravel road for 1.2 miles to the state line.

You will begin seeing yellow blazes along the road but continue driving until the yellow trail goes into the woods on the right. At this point, you will also see blue blazes (the Connecticut trails are marked in blue). On the left side of the road is a concrete post that designates the state boundary. There is room enough for three or four cars to be parked on the right shoulder.

Trail

At the start, as you enter the woods on the right side of the road, you will be following both yellow and blue blazes as this segment runs virtually on the state line. Immediately, you begin passing through the laurel thickets that remain green all year and blossom spectacularly in June.

You'll also see the boulders, ledges, and outcroppings. Rocks are everywhere. With the right side of the trail posted, take some time looking over the ledges on the left. Short side paths lead to some intriguing formations. In about ½ mile, the trail forks, the blue blazes curving left and the yellow going right. For now, take the yellow path (it also has blue blazes for a short distance; they represent a Scout trail that curls back toward the camp). As the trail drops into a small ravine, look for a side path going right; it leads to a cavelike chamber under an outcropping. Back on the yellow trail, follow it until it climbs one of the larger stone ridges. This outcropping is considered the southern terminus of the Tippecansett Trail. By continuing north on the Tippecansett, you could walk all the way to Beach Pond and then on to the many trails of the Arcadia Management Area. For this walk, however, turn around here, return to the blue blazes, and head into Connecticut.

The trail climbs over boulders and ridges and soon reaches one of the rushing little streams. This is a place for another short detour. Instead of simply crossing on the plank bridge, take a few minutes and follow a path upstream (to the right) from the bridge. Quickly, you'll reach another immense outcropping with numerous crevices and cracks that

Stonework from a vanished mill on Narragansett Trail.

demand exploration. Also, you may be amazed that the tiny brook only a few feet wide at the bridge here opens into a wide and lovely marsh. The giant rock provides a great place from which to look over the marsh, and even though you are still early in your walk, you may find yourself lingering here for some time.

When you're ready to resume walking, return to the little bridge and follow the blue blazes west. This next segment, after the scramble up from the bridge, is easier than the first, running through a flatter section of woods that is liberally sprinkled with laurel. When the going becomes rocky again, about ½ mile from where the brook crosses, you are nearing another brook. Here, amid the boulders, are the intriguing stone remnants of a mill where wooden spools and bobbins were once turned. With some inspection, you can find a long, stone-lined tunnel that formerly carried water from the brook, through the mill, and back to the brook. Just below the mill site, the brook splashes through a lovely, and lively, little cascade.

Immediately beyond the stream, the trail breaks into a small clearing dominated by a three-sided log shelter used by overnight campers. In a few more minutes, the trail reaches a gravel lane. You have now walked approximately 2¼ miles and are nearing Green Falls Pond. You have three choices: follow the lane left to a dike at the edge of the pond, take the blue path down to the water and then turn left, or circle the entire pond to the right, passing a beach and picnic area on the way.

The lane to the left is the shortest route but not the prettiest. I suggest staying on the blue trail. It goes to the right on the lane for a short distance, then turns left and follows another rocky brook down toward the pond. Just before reaching the water, the trail divides again. An orange-blazed path goes to the right, and a sign indicates that a full loop of the pond would get you to the dam above the ravine in 1.2 miles. If you have the time and energy, do it. The route includes more boulders and laurel—more of a good thing—in addition to visiting the picnic area and beach.

For this walk, go left on the blue trail. Despite the dense laurel thickets, the trail provides some good views of the large but shallow pond, its rocky islands, and forested shores. You may see ducks or geese on the pond. I've seen loons here as well.

The trail emerges on an earthen dike built along the lower end of the pond. The lane you crossed earlier passes just below the dike, then curves into the forest and runs out to the gravel road you will walk later, but please do not take this shortcut. You would be cheating yourself out of the climax of this hike.

Instead, walk the length of the dike, then, at its far end, pick up the blue blazes again and follow them through a grove of hemlocks. The trail runs down to a stone and concrete dam with a wooden walkway. The blue trail remains on the near side, instead of going onto the dam, but before climbing down into the ravine, go out onto the walkway. On your right is the pond lapping placidly. But under your feet the water is spilling into a 35-foot falls.

The falls is even more impressive from below. Return to the blue trail (where you first reached the dam) and take it into the ravine. For many hikers, this ravine or gorge is the highlight of the Narragansett Trail. It is very narrow in places, with jagged rock walls looming on both sides. The tall hemlocks keep the gorge in almost-permanent shadow, casting every-thing—rocks, logs, roots, lichens, moss—in an eerie green.

But don't spend all your time looking up. The trail is a bit tricky because it clings to the shore of the brook and you have to negotiate numerous rocks and roots. As the gorge narrows and the brook goes into a series of drops, you even have to cross over to the right bank. When the water is low, this is a simple matter of stepping across the chute. When water is higher, you might have to find stepping stones. Or jump.

Once on the right bank, the trail soon flattens. It runs along the brook and passes a huge stone cairn, then emerges onto the gravel road. Here, the blue blazes turn right. You, however, need to turn left. Your car is parked just over 1 mile ahead. Normally, walking a mile on a road is an unappealing way to finish a hike, but because there are no houses and no utility wires along this road, and virtually no traffic, it's not hard to think of it as a wide woods path. There are plenty of stone walls, more brooks, and more hemlocks to enjoy.

12 · Browning Mill Pond-Roaring Brook

Walking distance: 2¼ miles
Walking time: 1½ hours

For a good look at some of the recent improvements to the big Arcadia Wildlife Management Area in Exeter, as well as some reminders of the past, try this scenic walk around the Browning Mill Pond, with a side loop to a beautiful little fishing pond on Roaring Brook. This is an easy walk suitable for giving children a taste of hiking and can be easily trimmed to 1½ miles. The ambitious can extend the walk if they wish because this route connects with other trails.

On this walk you'll get to see, in addition to two of the most idyllic ponds in the area, a footbridge and fishing pier built for the handicapped, the remains of a long-abandoned stone pavilion, old concrete dams and sluice gates, and rectangular ponds left over from a fish hatchery. You'll also see a tumbling brook, a picnic area, and a beach and will walk through attractive forest.

Nearly all of the trail is flat and easy, although rocks and roots make you pay attention to your footing in a few places. There is no "bad" season for walking here, but spring and fall might be best. The beach area and parking lot are often busy on summer weekends.

Access

As with other trails in the Arcadia Management Area, take RI 165 (Ten Rod Road) west from RI 3. Turn left onto Arcadia Road and look for the Browning Mill Pond Recreation Area about 2 miles from RI 165. Go past the beach area and enter the large parking lot on your right.

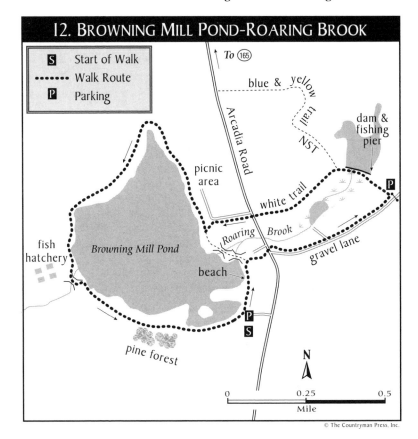

12. BROWNING MILL POND-ROARING BROOK

S Start of Walk
•••••• Walk Route
P Parking

To (165)

blue & yellow trail

Arcadia Road

dam & fishing pier

NST

picnic area

white trail

P

fish hatchery

Browning Mill Pond

Roaring Brook

gravel lane

beach

P
S

pine forest

N

0   0.25   0.5
Mile

© The Countryman Press, Inc.

Trail

I recommend parking at the far end of the lot; your return will be through pines along the left shore of the pond. Begin your walk by following a path that runs behind the beach area, parallel to the road. If you want to walk only around the 46-acre mill pond, simply go beyond the beach and take two footbridges to the path that circles the pond. Doing this will make a walk of about 1½ miles but will miss the smaller pond and the fishing pier.

To include that segment, look for a gravel lane running up from the beach toward the road you drove earlier. It will take you past a boarded-up park building to the road. Here, take a detour of a few steps to your left for a look at Roaring Brook, which pours beneath the road in a noisy, rocky descent. It's one of the prettier brooks in the area.

When ready to resume, take a gravel lane that is virtually across the road from the boarded-up building. This lane quickly goes past a very small pond and continues for about ¼ mile to a cutoff lane going to the left just before a gate on the gravel lane. Here you will see yellow and blue trail blazes. The yellow paint indicates this is part of the Arcadia Trail that runs 7 miles from the park's main office building on Arcadia Road to Route 165. The blue marks and some rectangular signs show it is also part of the long North South Trail (NST) that stretches all the way across the state.

Take the cutoff to the left. It leads to the parking lot for the Upper Roaring Brook Handicapped Access Trail, built to provide those with wheelchairs access to a truly gorgeous pond. The pond, stocked with trout, is spectacular in all seasons. Beavers and otters frequently use the pond and ducks and herons can sometimes be seen here.

At the far end of the boardwalk, you have a choice. The blue and yellow blazes go straight ahead in the forest. The return to Browning Mill Pond is the white-blazed path going left. If you are traveling with children, it is probably best to take this path back to the pond. If you are looking to add more distance and more history, stay on the yellow path. You will go through a pine grove, then a section filled with briars, underbrush, and a complex of stone walls. The trail goes out nearly to the highway, then curves back inland. Just after crossing one of the stone walls, you can see a large brick chimney in the woods on the left. The chimney does not appear to be from a house or cabin and there is much speculation among hikers about its origin. Longtime residents of the area say the chimney was part of a bakery that once stood on the site. From the chimney, you can continue on the yellow trail to the road and then follow the pavement back to the left (a fairly long walk), or you can backtrack to the fishing pond and then take the white trail to the road.

Those who walk the white trail will hear Roaring Brook roar before they reach the road. Go directly across the road or go a few steps to the left

Walkers are discovering the beauty of Browning Mill Pond.

to the brook and follow it down toward the large pond. Either route will take you to a picnic area near the shore. From there, look for a path going to the right at the edge of the water. At present, there are some faded yellow blazes along the first part of this path but most of the way is unmarked.

This path is rocky in places and can be muddy, although footbridges and plank walkways carry you over the wettest areas. You will follow this path all the way around the pond. At times it swings a short distance from the water, and dense foliage can obscure the views, but it always returns to the shore.

The path is smoother as you go along the far side of the pond and it is in this area you reach the abandoned stone pavilion. The walls are still standing but the roof has collapsed. You also begin seeing more stone walls in this section and you soon reach the concrete dam and sluice gates that once controlled water flow to mills. The path enables you to walk directly to the dam but you will have to retreat a few steps to take the trail that goes down to footbridges over the outlets from the pond.

Shortly beyond the dam you will come to an open area. To your right are a series of rectangular ponds, now mostly overgrown, that were part of a fish hatchery several years ago. The trail quickly curls to the left onto a dike built for the pond. Here, with the pond on your left, and a wooden fence and the old hatchery area on your right, are some of the best views of this walk. It is a good place to linger.

At the end of the dike you cross another bridge over abandoned sluice gates, then go through a pine forest. When the trail returns to the very edge of a small cove covered with lily pads, you are nearing the end. The path will take you directly into the parking lot and your car.

13 · John B. Hudson Trail

Walking distance: 3½ miles
Walking time: 2 hours

The John B. Hudson Trail, named for one of Rhode Island's hiking pioneers, is one of the oldest in the state trail system and one of the shortest, yet it remains one of the most popular. It should be; it's a gem.

It is about 1½ miles long each way, running from RI 165 to Breakheart Pond in the Arcadia Wildlife Management Area in Exeter and back, but sections of it are downright dazzling, particularly in late spring, when the thickets of mountain laurel are in bloom, and in winter, when the gurgling stream that it follows for a while is as pretty as any picture with ice and snow. Two features formerly found on this trail, an observation tower and a footbridge, are gone. Both were dismantled when they became unsafe.

The trail, in addition to the natural beauty of the forest and the brook, still offers a look at a tiny cemetery, the cellar of a long-vanished house, and, at Breakheart Pond, a concrete fish ladder. All in all, it packs a lot of highlights into a round trip of about 3½ miles.

Part of the region's vast Yellow-Dot Trail system maintained by the Appalachian Mountain Club, the Hudson links with the Breakheart Trail (Walk 17), so extending this walk is easy.

The trail loops as it nears Breakheart Pond, and a white-blazed path allows you to begin your return by following picturesque Breakheart Brook. And, rather than simply retracing your steps back on the first segment, I suggest returning on a woods road that adds a pleasant area that includes the cellar hole.

This walk is a good one for giving children a taste of hiking. Most of it is flat and easy, although a bit rocky in places. Also, the middle segment

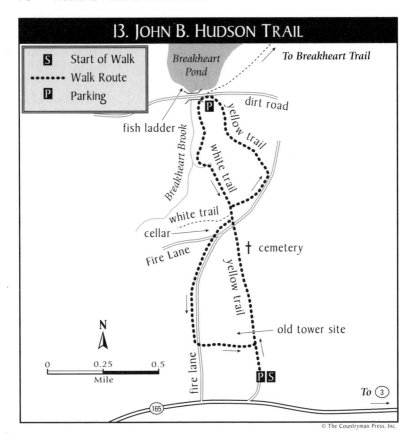

13. John B. Hudson Trail

S Start of Walk
••••• Walk Route
P Parking

Breakheart Pond

To Breakheart Trail

dirt road

yellow trail

fish ladder

Breakheart Brook

white trail

white trail

cellar

Fire Lane

† cemetery

yellow trail

old tower site

N

0   0.25   0.5
Mile

fire lane

P S

To ③

165

© The Countryman Press, Inc.

will involve some scrambling up and down steep slopes along the stream. That area is sometimes muddy and the footing can be treacherous, particularly in early spring, so it might be best to wait until late May or June. Fortunately, that's when the laurel is in bloom.

Access

To reach the start, take RI 165 2.6 miles west from RI 3. The entrance lane, on the right, is marked by a sign. The lane angles back to a parking area that is veiled from the highway by trees.

Trail

Almost immediately after leaving the parking area, the trail forks. Go to the left, with the yellow blazes. You'll be heading slightly uphill into a grove of pines. At the *second* side path going off to the left, where young pines crowd the trail, you can detour to the site of the old observation tower that once provided a panoramic view of the area, before the surrounding trees outgrew the tower. At this writing only rubble remains of the tower. You will be finishing your walk by climbing this ridge from the opposite side.

Back on the yellow trail, you'll pass beneath towering pines and go through the first of many laurel thickets on this route. When the timing is right, late spring, this can be a stroll through a virtual tunnel of fragrant pink and white blossoms.

About ¾ mile from your start, shortly after crossing a low stone wall, you'll reach the little family graveyard, surrounded by stone walls, just to the right of the trail. The few legible dates on the tombstones range from the 1830s to the 1850s.

Just beyond the cemetery the trail crosses a fire lane known as Tripp Trail, which you will later walk in two directions. For now, take the yellow trail across the road. In a few yards, you reach an intersection. The yellow trail turns right, a white-blazed path goes directly ahead, and another white path goes to the left. Take the yellow trail; you'll return on the white trail that is directly ahead. The yellow trail quickly emerges on the wider woods road but follows it only briefly before cutting back into the pines. It then climbs a ridge and weaves its way downhill toward Breakheart Pond.

The trail leaves the forest at a parking area beside the pond. A bridge and the old fish ladder are just to your left. (For a description of the ladder and Breakheart Pond, see Walk 17.) This is a good spot for a break, but when you're ready to resume walking, look for a white-blazed trail running back along the near side of the brook, through a narrow fence opening. This is a particularly lovely segment to walk. The trail alternately

Quiet forest paths make up the Hudson walk.

hugs the rocky, rushing stream and veers away through dense laurel thickets. At one point you'll find yourself at the top of a decaying wooden stairway that formerly led to a footbridge. You could go down here for a close look at the brook, but there will be spots ahead where the trail itself is virtually on the banks.

Where the trail dips near the water, the going can be muddy and slippery, but the placement of many stepping stones has greatly improved the situation. After about ½ mile of following the stream, the trail makes an abrupt left turn and climbs the slope, going up a seasonal brook, and then reaches the junction you passed earlier.

Here, leave the white trail, which turns to your right, and rejoin the yellow trail straight ahead, but follow it only the few yards to Tripp Trail, the open fire lane. Take this road to the right. It is easy to walk and delightful to look at, with many tumbling stone walls and overhanging trees. You will soon see another road coming in from the right, and in the corner where the fire lanes meet is the cellar hole. It is hidden in a tangle of bushes, including old forsythias that continue to bloom each spring.

Stay on the woods road for about ½ mile, until reaching the side path that takes you to the old tower site and back to your car. Finding this cut-off can be tricky, however. It is on the left at a point where the road makes a gentle curve to the right, just beyond an unusually big pine on the right shoulder. The road widens a bit here and is flanked with young pines. At present, the path is marked with a small stone cairn, but cairns are not permanent. This path, if you can find it, will take you up a steep slope to the tower site. From there, it's a short walk back to the yellow trail and then less than ¼ mile to the right to your car.

If you happen to miss this cutoff, simply stay on the woods road to its end at RI 165; it's also less than ¼ mile. Then turn left to reach your car.

14 · Mount Tom Trail

Walking distance: 5½ miles
Walking time: 2½ to 3 hours

This walk up and over Mount Tom in Exeter features a wide variety of attractions. Along the way you'll stroll through a thriving reforestation project, cross rushing trout streams, and pause atop rocky cliffs with long panoramic views.

As a bonus, you can shorten your walk without retracing your steps, if so desired, by walking a highway back to your car. Walk this entire 5½-mile loop, however, and you will avoid the paved road, except for the few steps it takes to cross it twice. You will be returning along quiet dirt roads that offer excellent chances for seeing wildlife.

Spring is a great time to walk this trail. It's picturesque in fall, too, but you may run into numerous hunters then. If recommending one time, however, I would suggest June, when the abundant mountain laurel that crowds the trail in places is in its full glory.

Access

Mount Tom Trail, another of the many Appalachian Mountain Club (AMC) paths in the Arcadia Wildlife Management Area, officially begins along RI 165 at a spot known as Appie Crossing about 2.5 miles west of RI 3, almost across from the John B. Hudson Trail (Walk 13). There is little parking space at Appie Crossing, however, and returning there would mean a walk along heavily used RI 165 or retracing part of your route. Instead, I recommend driving another mile (3.5 miles from RI 3) to the Arcadia Check Station and Canoe Access, on the left, just after crossing a bridge over the Wood River. Park at the far end of the lot; the white-blazed Mount Tom Trail goes into the woods from the parking area.

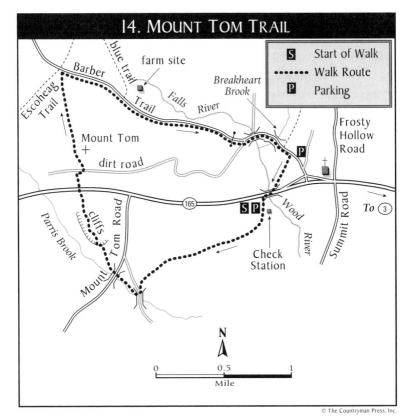

14. MOUNT TOM TRAIL

S Start of Walk
•••••• Walk Route
P Parking

Barber Trail
blue trail
farm site
Escoheag Trail
Breakheart Brook
Falls
River
Mount Tom +
dirt road
Frosty Hollow Road
P
Parris Brook
cliffs
Mount Tom Road
165
S **P**
Wood River
Check Station
Summit Road
To ③

N

0   0.5   1
Mile

© The Countryman Press, Inc.

Trail

As soon as you enter the woods, you will be walking through a pine forest that was planted after 8,000 acres of timberland were destroyed in 1951 in one of the worst forest fires in Rhode Island history. Thousands of pines now thrive throughout this region and all the scars from that tragic fire have vanished.

The wide, open path is often flanked with wildflowers and you are likely to find deer tracks in the sandy soil (in fall and early winter, this area teems with hunters). Drawing more attention, though, will be the numerous anthills. Some are huge. Visit on a hot, sunny day, and you may find the ground covered with industrious ants.

When the trail emerges onto a gravel lane, the white blazes go left a short distance, then re-enter the woods on the right near a small stream. This stream is Parris Brook and it is lovely, with numerous small waterfalls over man-made dams that were constructed to enhance the trout fishing. This segment is so pleasant you may be sorry when it ends at a paved road, but the highlight of the hike—both figuratively and literally—is just ahead.

The trail crosses Mount Tom Road, goes into the forest, and begins climbing. Once, a lane ran up this part of the slope, but now brush has virtually obliterated it. Still, if you look closely, you can find some stone embankments and walls that reveal the original route.

Within minutes you will be straddling a ridge. Cutoff paths lead to rock ledges, and the higher you climb, the more ledge you find and the better the views. From these overlooks, whether facing east or west, you can see for miles, and the scenery is virtually all forest. It is hard to believe this is densely populated Rhode Island—it strongly resembles New Hampshire. In early fall, the valley below is a patchwork quilt of reds, yellows, and greens. In spring, green of various shades dominates, with an occasional dogwood in blossom adding a dash of white. Go in June, when the mountain laurel is in bloom, and the pink and white blossoms may demand as much of your attention as the long views.

The trail along the ridge is almost all rock. The adventurous and nimble can take shortcuts up and over the boulders. The less agile should follow the trail around the huge rocks. Both routes wind up at the same places—at the top of outcroppings that drop straight off. It would be a long fall, so watch your step. At the bottom of some cliffs rest great slabs of stone chopped off by the glaciers. The high outlooks are about 1¼ miles from your start.

More up-and-down scrambling is ahead, but fewer open vistas, and shortly you begin descending to RI 165. The final descent is abrupt. One moment you feel you are in wilderness; the next, you are on a busy highway. At this point you've walked just over 2 miles. If you want, you can return to your car by simply turning right and following the highway. It is less than a mile back to the parking lot.

Mountain Laurel is part of the attraction on Mount Tom.

But Mount Tom itself is still ahead. The trail crosses the highway, a few yards to the left, and immediately starts upward. However, there are fewer rocks, no cliffs, and no overlooks on this section of the trail. For the most part it is an easy but uneventful walk up and over the crest, which at 460 feet is one of the highest spots in the area. Unlike most hills, it is difficult to tell when you are at the summit.

After the initial climb, the trail crosses a woods lane (which could be taken to the right, although it would cut off the wildlife road) and then runs straight and fairly level for nearly a mile. The trail is deeply eroded in places from years of use by hikers and bikers, but it also features virtual tunnels through dense stands of mountain laurel. Again, timing is critical. When the laurel is flowering, these tunnels are delightful. At other times, they are simply thick bushes.

The trail ends on the dirt road called Barber Trail. Just to the left, the Escoheag Trail (Walk 15) crosses the road and some hikers link the two walks. To return to your car, however, turn right and follow the open road.

It runs about 2 miles, mostly downhill, passing plenty of forest scenes and game management fields, eventually crossing two streams (Falls River and Breakheart Brook) that merge shortly below here to form the Wood River. In spring this is a delightful walk with a great deal of bird activity and numerous flowers growing on the shoulders of the old road. It is one of the better places for finding the tiny but fragrant trailing arbutus.

Near an old farmstead site (look for a parking area on the left), about ½ mile down this dirt road, you will see blue blazes going off to the left. These blazes signify that the North South Trail cuts through here on its way from the coast to the Massachusetts border. The blue blazes also run ahead along this road and you can follow them much of the rest of the way.

The old farm site is a good resting place—you've gone just under 4 miles at this point. In spring several old apple trees still blossom and lilac bushes bloom. In June, the place is colorful with flowering multiflora roses and many wildflowers such as hawkweeds and daisies.

When you're ready to resume walking, keep an eye on the fields to the left. They are usually planted in grains that attract wildlife. I've seen wild turkeys in these fields and tracks on the sandy road show that deer often cross to the fields. Butterflies and dragonflies usually accompany you if you walk this road in warm weather.

About ¾ mile from the farm site, you will reach, in quick succession, a gate, the woods lane coming in from the right, and a stream bridge. Cross the bridge and turn right, still following the blue blazes. You'll soon reach another bridge, very popular with fishermen.

Beyond this second bridge you need to watch your landmarks. Stay on the main road when the blue trail turns left. In a few more yards, just before reaching a large parking lot, look for a gated lane on your right. A sign just beyond the gate identifies this as Hargraves Trail. Take it, and in ¼ mile you will reach RI 165 beside a bridge. Cross the bridge, turn left on a gravel lane, and you are back at your car.

15 · Escoheag Trail

Walking distance: 3¼ miles
Walking time: 2 hours

Escoheag Trail is a pleasant, scenic path on its own, but it can serve equally well as a warm-up for hikes to other favorite Rhode Island hiking destinations. The 3¼-mile loop described here wanders through a rocky forest, then returns along an unpaved woods road. Partway through the loop, the ambitious can make a detour to Mount Tom (Walk 14) and its panoramic views, and at this walk's far end hikers can easily extend their tour by going up to Penny Hill on the Breakheart Trail (Walk 17) or by following a stream to lovely Stepstone Falls on the Ben Utter Trail (Walk 16).

Features of Escoheag include an old picnic area with an imposing stone pavilion hidden in the woods, numerous little brooks that tumble through the woodland, and a couple of ledges that must be climbed and crossed. The same features, however, that make this trail inviting also make it a bit strenuous in the early going.

Access

To reach the start of Escoheag, take RI 165 west about 5.5 miles from RI 3, turn right on Escoheag Hill Road, and continue for 1 mile. Turn right on a gravel lane next to an abandoned log building. This is the old Beach Pond State Recreation Area, now used chiefly by bikers, horseback riders, hikers, and, in season, hunters and fishers. Park in the lot to the right of the building.

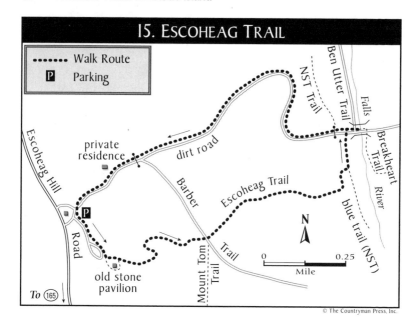

15. Escoheag Trail

Walk Route
P Parking

private residence

dirt road

NST Trail

Ben Utter Trail

Falls

Breakheart Trail

River

Escoheag Trail

Escoheag Hill Road

P

Barber

Mount Tom Trail

old stone pavilion

To 165

N

blue trail (NST)

0   0.25
Mile

© The Countryman Press, Inc.

Trail

You'll see a small sign for the Escoheag Trail on a tree and white blazes
going to the right along a gravel lane just beyond the parking area. This
lane runs to what was a picnic grounds, and a few fireplaces remain. At the
end of this lane, the white blazes run off to the left, into the forest, and
begin dropping down between boulders.

In moments, though, you'll notice a building above you on the right,
perched on a high outcropping. This is the stone-sided shelter left over
from the days when this was a popular weekend spot known as the Ledges
Picnic Area. Side trails run up to the pavilion, and it is worth the climb. In
winter and after leaves have dropped in fall, it provides an excellent view
of the surrounding woodland.

When you're ready to resume your hike, climb down the ledge, but be
sure to find, among all the unmarked paths, the white-blazed Escoheag
Trail. It goes to the left, almost directly away from the ledge on which the
shelter stands. You will be passing through oak and beech groves, going

Old stone pavilion still looms above Escoheag Trail.

through laurel thickets, and climbing up and over rocky ledges. In spring and rainy periods there are several little brooks that must be crossed, but all can be managed easily because of footbridges and numerous stepping stones. In spring, the place is active with forest birds—thrushes, vireos, ovenbirds—and you are likely to see numerous chipmunks.

After topping the second major ridge beyond the old shelter, you'll notice "Private Property" signs just to the right of the trail. Soon the terrain begins flattening. About 1 mile from your start, you will emerge on a dirt road. Just to your right are white blazes and a sign for the Mount Tom Trail. Taking that trail, across Route 165, would take you to some of the better cliffs in Rhode Island; a detour there and back to this spot would add about 3¼ miles to your walk.

The Escoheag Trail goes directly across the dirt road, known as Barber Trail, and runs mostly downhill for more than ½ mile. The footing is still rocky in places but the walking is easy. When you start seeing pine trees, you are nearing an old lane that will take you out of this forest. On the old lane, you'll see blue blazes that indicate it is part of the long North

South Trail (NST). You go left and in minutes reach another gravel road. This is the road you later will walk back to your car, to the left, but first go to the right. The river is just a few yards away.

This is the Falls River, one of the most attractive waterways in the state. Just before the bridge, on the left side of the road, is the start of the Ben Utter Trail, which leads to Stepstone Falls (see Walk 16 for a description of this trail). That trail is blazed in yellow along with blue for the North South Trail. A walk to the falls and back would add about 3 miles to your hike. Across the bridge, on the right, is the start of the Breakheart Trail. If you take it up to Penny Hill and back, following yellow blazes, you will walk an additional 1¼ miles or so.

Even if you take neither extension, the rushing stream is a good place for a break. It is a clear, noisy stream that features natural and man-made waterfalls that cater to trout and fishermen. The river is a scenic place to linger in all seasons.

As you start up the road back toward your car, you will notice more blue North South Trail blazes going up the road, then turning onto to a woods lane, on the right, just beyond a gate. These blue blazes lead horseback riders and bicyclists who are doing the North South Trail to another abandoned picnic grounds and, eventually, to Stepstone Falls. Riders are asked not to travel on the fragile footpath along the river.

The gate on the main road prohibits cars and trucks from using this road except during hunting and fishing seasons. The road is easy to walk, although the grade is quite steep where it makes a horseshoe bend to the right. Forest crowds in on both sides, numerous seasonal brooks trickle underneath, and stone walls wander through the woods at seemingly random angles. On days when there is no other traffic, this road is as delightful to walk as a wilderness path. I once met a red fox on this road; it was carrying a chipmunk and appeared to be heading home to feed its family.

You will pass a dirt road going to the left (this is Barber Trail, which you crossed earlier), then another gate that regulates traffic, and a private residence. After that, it's just a few more steps to your car beside the old park building.

16 · Ben Utter Trail

Walking distance: 3½ miles
Walking time: 2 hours

The Ben Utter Trail is perfect for walkers who prefer thinking of their time moving through the forest as a relaxing pastime and as a means of viewing the handiwork of both nature and humans rather than an endurance test. This trail, named for one of the pioneers of the Rhode Island trail system, is short, relatively easy, and very accommodating. Wooden bridges span the brooks and stone steps ease your way up and down some of the steeper slopes.

Following the aptly named Falls River upstream, this trail passes the remains of an old gristmill and a sawmill, leads through thickets of mountain laurel and dense growths of ferns, and culminates at Stepstone Falls, one of Rhode Island's most beautiful inland spots. It also provides a look at an abandoned picnic area that once was very popular but now is virtually forgotten. The trail runs between two dirt roads in the Exeter portion of the Arcadia Wildlife Management Area and links with the Escoheag Trail (Walk 15), so your day can be easily extended if desired. It is also part of the long North South Trail that runs the entire length of Rhode Island.

The route described here goes to Stepstone Falls, then loops up to the former picnic area, and follows a woods road before returning to the river.

Access

To reach the start, take RI 165 west from RI 3 about 3 miles to Frosty Hollow Road. Look for the white West Exeter Baptist Church at the corner. Turn right onto the gravel road and drive to its end at a T-intersection.

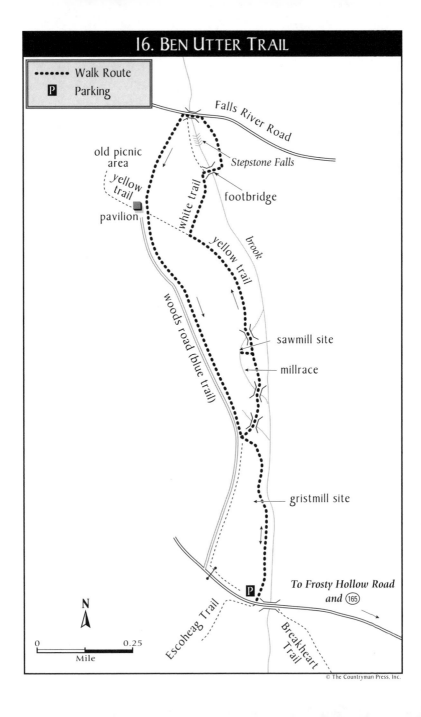

16. BEN UTTER TRAIL

Legend:
- ••••••• Walk Route
- P Parking

Falls River Road

old picnic area

yellow trail

pavilion

white trail

Stepstone Falls

footbridge

brook

yellow trail

woods road (blue trail)

sawmill site

millrace

gristmill site

To Frosty Hollow Road and (165)

P

Escoheag Trail

Breakheart Trail

N

0   0.25
Mile

© The Countryman Press, Inc.

Go left about 2¼ miles until you cross the river. Park just beyond the bridge, on the right, where you will see yellow blazes indicating the trail.

Trail

The trail, blazed in blue for the North South Trail (NST) as well as yellow, runs virtually on the riverbank at its start. You will immediately see and hear the first falls, although in this section they are man-made structures—huge logs anchored by rocks—installed years ago to make the stream more attractive to trout. The tumbling waters add a pleasing, soothing overtone to your walk.

After crossing a small brook on a wooden bridge, the trail goes left over a ridge that once was part of an earthen dam built for a gristmill. Stone steps lead both up the ridge and back down. Other stonework from the vanished mill is visible around the ridge and on the opposite side of the river.

As the trail passes a barway, you will momentarily break out onto a wider woods lane now used mostly by horseback riders. The blue blazes run along this lane, which you could walk to the former picnic area and then to Stepstone Falls, but in doing so you would miss most of the river scenes. However, take note of the barway, which is actually a guardrail; you will need to recognize it on your return walk.

Instead, stay on the yellow trail, swinging back into the woods on the right immediately after reaching the lane. Here, you'll enter a thicket of mountain laurel, the shrub that covers the trail with pink and white blossoms in June. There is one short bridge in the thicket, and when you cross the next bridge (your third since the start) you are entering a most interesting area. The brook under this bridge was dug as a millrace for a vertical sawmill powered by a waterwheel. Off the trail to the left you can see what remains of the mill, a rubble of huge stone slabs. Many of these stones have fallen into the water but it is not difficult to picture the effort that went into building the mill and digging the channel through the rocky ground. Another few yards takes you to still another bridge, again crossing the millrace, and off to the right you can see part of the dam

Stepstone Falls is the highlight of Ben Utter Trail.

that was built to divert water from the river to the mill. It's a good spot to linger.

Up to this point you are continually within earshot of the water, and the moods of the little river can make each walk here seem different. I have seen the river roaring over the falls in a frothy fury and I've seen it gurgling in a gentle lullaby. It all depends on the season, the water level, and the rainfall in previous days. Angry or serene, the many falls offer plenty of excuses for pauses.

Eventually, the path curves to the left, away from the river, and begins climbing. But just as you feel you are finally leaving the water behind you will reach a white-blazed trail breaking off to the right. Take this trail. If you remain on the yellow trail, you will go directly into the old picnic ground, but save that for later. For now, take the white trail back to the river.

Footing on the white path is very rocky, and there may be some muddy areas, but it is only about ¼ mile to a footbridge just below Stepstone Falls. This is another wonderful place to linger. The water sweeps over the flat, steplike stones that gave the place its name. Some of the falls are natural, others were created by a quarrying operation that took place long ago.

Cross the footbridge and follow the white trail as it runs along the far side of the river, passing stone slabs that were cut out of the river but never used, and emerges onto a dirt road (Falls River Road). Here, turn left, cross the road bridge, and return to the woods. You will see blazes in both yellow and blue on a trail that angles uphill, away from the river.

Follow the blue and yellow trail; it will take you to an old log pavilion at the forgotten picnic area. A few other buildings remain, too, along with what is left of the paved road that once brought in dozens of picnickers on summer weekends.

At the pavilion, you'll see yellow blazes going both right and left. Left takes you back to the river. Right goes through the picnic area toward another trail that eventually runs out to Beach Pond on Route 165. Blue blazes also go to the right briefly, then turn left when they reach the old picnic grounds road. You can follow the blue blazes all the way back to your car if you wish. They follow the old pavement for a while, then turn left onto a dirt lane that runs less than 100 yards from where you parked, and it is pleasant enough.

I suggest, however, taking the blue trail less than a mile, until reaching the barway-guardrail where you originally left the blue blazes on your way upriver. I invariably find myself returning to the yellow trail that runs back to the river. That splashing sound is hard to resist.

17 · Breakheart Trail

Walking distance: 6½ miles
Walking time: 2½ to 3 hours

Breakheart Pond is a picturesque place that has been popular with Rhode Island outdoorspeople for decades. This 6½-mile walk loops halfway around the pond, then adds a more strenuous hike through dense forest to an abandoned youth camp complex. The walk ends with a stroll along a little-used woods road. Don't let the idea of walking on a road dissuade you; many times walks along roads like this are very rewarding, particularly if you like wildlife. You will see more birds and mammals along rural roads than in dense forests, where the foliage is too thick and the walking too noisy.

This is another walk in the state-owned Arcadia Wildlife Management Area in Exeter and West Greenwich. The yellow-blazed trail connects with the John B. Hudson Trail (Walk 13) at one end and can be extended to the Ben Utter Trail (Walk 16) and Escoheag Trail (Walk 15) at the other, so lengthening your hike is easy.

In several ways, Breakheart Trail has improved in recent years, particularly with the replacing of rickety bridges with solid new ones. However, there are negatives as well: dirt bikers have carved their own paths through the area and can make finding your route a bit confusing in places, and the old camp buildings are deteriorating rapidly and may not last much longer. Still, it's a walk worth taking. At the start of your route you can examine an old fish ladder and a small cellar hole. The pond and streams are lovely in all seasons, you'll pass through magnificent pine and beech groves, and you'll perhaps see several forms of wildlife ranging from chipmunks and squirrels to grouse, deer, beaver, coyote, or wild turkey.

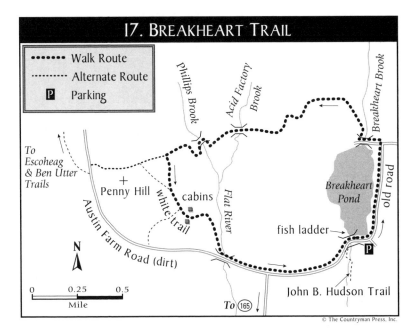

17. BREAKHEART TRAIL

•••••• Walk Route
·········· Alternate Route
P   Parking

Phillips Brook

Acid Factory Brook

Breakheart Brook

To
Escoheag
& Ben Utter
Trails

+ Penny Hill

white trail

cabins

Flat River

Breakheart Pond

old road

fish ladder

Austin Farm Road (dirt)

N

0   0.25   0.5
Mile

To (165)

John B. Hudson Trail

P

© The Countryman Press, Inc.

Access

To reach Breakheart Pond, take RI 165 exactly 3 miles west of RI 3. Turn right (north) at the West Exeter Baptist Church on gravel Frosty Hollow Road, continue 1.5 miles to its end, then go right on another gravel road until it ends at the pond. Cross the bridge over Breakheart Brook and park just beyond it.

Trail

Before starting your walk, look over the dam and concrete fish ladder beside the parking area. The fish ladder, a series of shallow, rectangular pools, was built to help trout get over the dam and return upstream to spawn. Although broken in places now and of little use to fish, it is one of the few such ladders remaining in the state. Also, go up onto the earthen dam for a look at the pond. Popular with fishermen, it also draws water-fowl during migration periods and occasionally you may see an otter, beaver, or muskrat swimming about. The pond, as well as Breakheart Brook and Breakheart Road, derive their names from nearby Breakheart Hill, which got its name from the heartbreaking task of driving oxen and horses up its slopes long ago.

To follow Breakheart Trail, follow the old road to the right from the parking area past a gate, then turn left on a narrower lane that appears to circle the pond. At this corner, on the left, is the small cellar hole. There are numerous stone walls through this area as well, showing that this was once farmland. You will cross the first of many brooks in this segment and walk beneath towering trees, mostly pines.

At the far end of the pond you reach another junction; go left, crossing another bridge almost immediately. Often there are beaver signs in this area. You could follow this road all the way around the pond, making an easy 1½-mile stroll, but the yellow trail turns to the right, into the woods, just a few steps beyond the bridge.

The trail follows the brook briefly, then angles uphill through dense forest. There are plenty of rocks but the footing is not difficult. Pines and oaks are the dominant trees, and the number of squirrels and chipmunks in the area increase accordingly. Years ago, while walking this loop, my young son counted 22 chipmunks and 12 squirrels.

You will cross a couple of unmarked paths; ignore them. Before going 2 miles from your start, you'll emerge on an old woods road; here the yellow-blazed trail turns left for a few steps, then goes back into the woods on the right. Now, as you begin heading downhill, you can see, through trees on the right, signs marking the boundary of the University of Rhode Island's (URI) research area called the W. Alton Jones Campus. There is no trespassing in the research forest, but if you walk over close enough to read the signs you'll notice a motorcycle path running along the boundary.

The trail weaves and wanders for a while, and you will cross the cycle path, but following the yellow blazes is not difficult. You come closest to the URI property line at a bridge over a lovely stream with a most unflattering name, Acid Factory Brook. Here, be careful. Just beyond this bridge,

Stone chimney awaits walkers on Breakheart Trail.

the yellow trail angles left (a wider path goes straight ahead, up a hill; it is a cycle trail and would lead you astray). The yellow trail is blazed well and you should have no trouble staying on the proper route.

The trail follows the brook briefly, then curves right and begins climbing into a dense pine forest. Often described in the past as "parklike" because of the tall pines and little understory, this grove is now in transition with thousands of young pines filling the forest floor and competing to replace the aging generation still standing above. At a Y-fork in this grove, the yellow trail goes left and quickly reaches another brook, this one crossed on a two-log bridge. This bridge is roughly 3½ miles from your start.

For the next ½ mile or so, the going is flat and easy, through mixed forest, but keep an eye out for your next turn. Just before the yellow trail starts up a rocky slope, you should see a white-blazed trail on the left and a sign saying Shelter Trail. This narrow path, decorated in spring with abundant wildflowers called trailing arbutus, will take you to the old youth camp complex. (The yellow trail goes up to a summit called Penny

Hill, then down the other side and out to Austin Farm Road. After crossing the road it eventually connects with the beginning of the Ben Utter Trail and the end of the Escoheag Trail.)

The white-blazed side trail, after about 1 mile, emerges at a junction of dirt roads. The blazes turn left but before going that way you might want to walk the unmarked lane straight ahead. It leads into part of the old Beach Pond Camps complex. Once a bustling little village in summer, it is now a place of silence. A few cabins remain but more have collapsed or been dismantled. Pines crowd in on all sides now and appear to be engulfing some of the cabins. Look carefully; old stone chimneys and other remains of the buildings are hidden in the surging young forest. When ready to continue your walk, return on the lane to where you left the white blazes and resume following them, now to your right. You will soon enter the main part of the complex, although fewer buildings remain here. The big dining hall that had been the center of camp activity was recently demolished, leaving little more than its huge fireplace and chimney. Hard to find, but still standing at this writing, is a rusting water tower. Now, trees tower above it and all but hide it from view.

Take the white trail out of the complex, down a steep hill, and out to Austin Farm Road. Turn left on the road. The white blazes quickly turn off, to the right, but for this walk stay on the road. You will pass Camp E-Hun-Tee, a private youth wilderness camp (out of sight on the left), and then Frosty Hollow Road, which you drove on your way to Breakheart Pond. From that junction, it is about ½ mile more back to the pond and your car.

18 · Pachaug Trail

Walking distance: 8½ miles
Walking time: 4 to 4½ hours

Build up to this walk. Try some of the shorter and easier trails first. The Pachaug will test your muscles and stamina. It's long—just over 8½ miles—and the first 5 miles are among the most strenuous segments in this book. But it's a most enjoyable walk and a beautiful one. You climb over rugged ledges in the first part, scrambling up and down ravines and clefts, crossing brooks, and then finishing with a few miles on flat old woods lanes.

This route is actually a combination of three hiking trails and runs a mile or more on an unmarked lane. You start in Rhode Island, swing around a pond into Connecticut, then return to Rhode Island past another pond and a spring. Along the way you can explore four old cellar holes and a family graveyard.

Access

To start, drive RI 165 about 7 miles west of RI 3 and I-95 to Beach Pond, which straddles the Rhode Island–Connecticut line. You can park beside the pond either in the large lot on the right side of the highway or in the smaller lot on the left side. In summer, it is wise to arrive early because not only is the hiking better at that time than in the heat of afternoon, but also because the parking areas can fill with swimmers, sunbathers, and fishermen.

Trail

The Pachaug is blazed in blue, but you also will see yellow blazes for the long Tippecansett Trail that runs for miles up the western edge of the state.

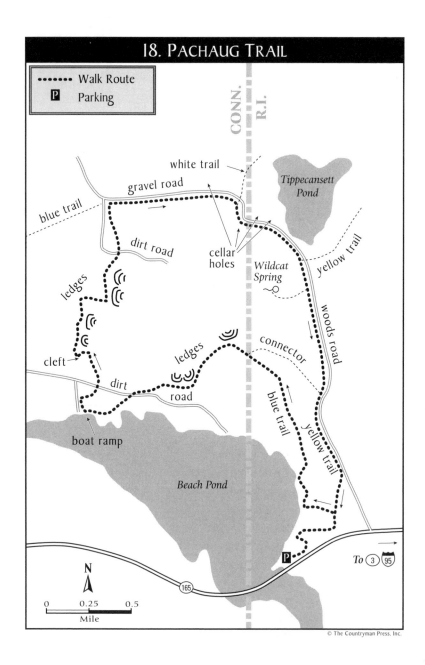

18. PACHAUG TRAIL

Legend:
- Walk Route
- P Parking

CONN. | R.I.

white trail

Tippecansett Pond

gravel road

blue trail

dirt road

cellar holes

Wildcat Spring

yellow trail

ledges

woods road

cleft

ledges

connector

dirt road

boat ramp

blue trail

yellow trail

Beach Pond

P

To ③ 95

N

0   0.25   0.5
Mile

© The Countryman Press, Inc.

The paths run together upon leaving the Beach Pond parking lot, and you will be returning on the Tippecansett.

From the parking area, go out to the highway and look for the blue and yellow blazes. The trail quickly goes into the woods and climbs a hill. This sets the tone for the first segment, which is very hilly and tends to loosen muscles for what lies ahead. In minutes, the trail swings back toward the pond, then it drops down a slope, crosses a gravel lane, and forks just beyond the lane. The yellow trail goes to the right, your blue route goes left.

The blue Pachaug path curls back toward the pond, twice going right down to the water's edge, before sweeping to the right through higher forest. You will quickly get a preview of the terrain ahead as the trail is rocky and hilly. And it continues getting rockier and hillier.

If the going appears too difficult, you have an option. At about 1¼ miles from the start, just after walking near a rocky brook and seeing rock piles scattered in the woods, you will reach a registration mailbox at the junction of a trail coming in from the right. This path, also blazed in blue, is a connector trail to the yellow Tippecansett Trail, and you can switch to that route.

Those staying on the blue trail will see a sign indicating that segments of the trail ahead will run through private property; walkers are asked to not wander off the trail. In the next section you cross into Connecticut, crossing brooks, skirting massive outcroppings, and walking beneath towering hemlocks. The ledges, many covered with mosses and lichens from permanent shading, are truly imposing, looming high above you. The trail runs at the base of many of these walls and occasionally clings partway up the rocks. The walking is not dangerous but requires care and attention, and therefore the going is likely to be slow. But places like this should not be hurried through anyway.

This rock-scrambling goes on for nearly 1 mile. Gradually you work your way down a slope and cross a dirt road. After another brief bit of up-and-down, you reach the pond's edge once more and then emerge on a boat landing. Here, you leave Beach Pond behind for the last time. You are about halfway through the strenuous section, or roughly 2½ miles into the hike.

To continue, walk across the parking lot to the point where the entrance road enters the lot. Here, the blue trail goes into the woods on the right. It climbs a ledge, then follows the edge of the parking lot before turning left (north). After crossing a dirt road, the trail levels off briefly. But don't be deceived; the most strenuous, but also most impressive, of the ledges are still ahead. Suddenly, the trail swings left and drops down a deep cleft that, to me, is the most spectacular spot in the entire 8½ miles. Walls tower above the cleft on both sides, and it is steep enough you'll probably have to use your hands in lowering yourself down. It is a great place to linger, perhaps while contemplating the might of the glaciers that helped create these formations.

Shortly beyond this cleft, as you climb out of a ravine, you reach a tricky spot. The blue trail makes a sharp left curve just as you reach a dirt-bike trail blazed in orange. Make sure you stay on the blue path. In a few yards it crosses the orange trail, and thereafter you will not see the orange trail again.

For some distance, the blue trail snakes back and forth along numerous other cliffs and ledges, nearly always running at the base of the high walls. This is wild terrain virtually untouched since the glaciers. You have to go up and around, over and down, the ledges, ravines, and boulders. The dense canopy of the hemlocks keeps the ground in permanent shade and there is little underbrush. Tiny red squirrels are common and birds can be heard overhead, but the area has an eerie, intriguing aura found along few other hikes in this book. Being here is worth all the effort the hiking requires.

Eventually, the trail starts climbing and weaves out of the hemlock outcropping area, entering a segment of laurel, hardwoods, and stone walls. You will reach an area where some logging has been done recently, then cross a grassy woods road and head slightly downhill through a forest with thousands of young pines. In another ⅓ mile or so, you emerge on the next road, a gravel one. At this point, you have gone just over 5 miles.

Pachaug Trail weaves past high rock walls.

The blue trail turns to the left, but for this walk, take the gravel road to the right. You should see white blazes along the road, for this is part of Connecticut's Canonicus Trail.

Your rock-climbing and ledge-viewing are finished. The rest of the walk is easy, but after the effort put forth, flat walking may be welcomed. Now you can experience new features. Shortly after turning onto the gravel road, look in the forest on the left for a cellar hole, the first of four along this road. Now this area is quiet and virtually forgotten, but the cellars show this was once a place where several families established homes.

As you round the second bend in the road, you will see the white blazes break off with a path to the left. Ignore them and stay on the road, which by now is more dirt than gravel. Where the road makes a 90-degree turn left, a lesser lane goes straight ahead. *Be sure to turn with the main road;* the other lane will lead you astray.

At this corner is the second cellar, and a short distance down the road to the left is the third, a large one. In another ¼ mile there is still another old foundation on the left; this one is still shaded by lilacs and surrounded by periwinkles, flowers that in spring are a vibrant living legacy to the vanished farmers.

In this segment you will pass a lane to the left and cross back into Rhode Island. Soon you are walking along the western side of Tippecansett Pond. There are few views of the water, however, and the land on the left is posted as private property. Be patient; up ahead is a spot where the lane runs near the water and you can get a good view. You will see some faded white blazes in this area and a few blue paint marks; ignore all of them and continue following the main road.

Shortly after passing the end of the pond, you will notice the yellow blazes of the Tippecansett Trail. The blazes turn off this road into the forest on the left but also run along the road ahead of you, which continues to be your route. For the remainder of this walk, you will be following the yellow blazes back toward Beach Pond.

In moments after rejoining the yellow trail, you will see a white-marked path on the right. This is the route to Wildcat Spring, which may or may not be worth the detour. It bubbles amid a pile of rocks in April and May, but there is not much to see in dry seasons. Still, it is a pleasant little path, and going to the spring and back will add only about ⅓ mile to your walk.

Back on the road, the yellow blazes will take you past a graveyard on the left. Still guarded by an iron gate and impressive stone walls, the graves date to the mid-1800s. Shortly beyond the cemetery, the yellow trail turns right and follows a narrower lane. You will notice white blazes going straight ahead on the road; they lead out to Route 165, so ignore them and stay on the yellow trail. Also ignore a blue-blazed trail, going to the right. It is the connector whose other end you passed at the mailbox several miles earlier.

Eventually, the yellow trail takes you to the spot where the yellow and blue blazes originally split. From here, a left turn and a climb up the slope will take you back to Beach Pond.

19 · Fisherville Brook Wildlife Refuge

Walking distance: 1¼ miles
Walking time: 1 to 1½ hours

This wildlife refuge in Exeter is becoming a favorite walking place. Owned and managed by the Audubon Society of Rhode Island, Fisherville Brook has several trails that loop and connect. The 1¼-mile route described here was the first trail created on the 900-acre property and, while visitors can now walk many miles through forests and old fields, this path is probably still the best in terms of beauty and interest.

The first section is an old lane that runs through a grove of majestic pines to a picturesque millpond. The second segment, a narrower footpath, circles the pond, passes pleasant meadows, and returns through another parklike pine grove. Remains of the mill stonework and bridges over streams add to the attractions.

Beavers live in the pond and otters are frequent visitors. Birds are often abundant both at the pond and around the meadows, where numerous birdhouses have been installed. Tiny red squirrels are often seen in the pines; chances are they'll greet you with their loud chatter.

Access

Drive RI 102 in Exeter to Widow Sweets Road (4 miles east of RI 3 and 3.2 miles west of RI 2). The Exeter town hall is at the intersection. Go north on Widow Sweets Road for 0.4 mile, then turn right onto Pardon Joslin Road and drive 0.7 mile. An Audubon Society sign and parking area are on the right. Two trails begin in the parking lot. A longer trail begins across the road, just down a driveway that leads to a private residence. That trail, blazed in red, circles through a mixed forest and can be added to the blue trail described here if you desire more exercise.

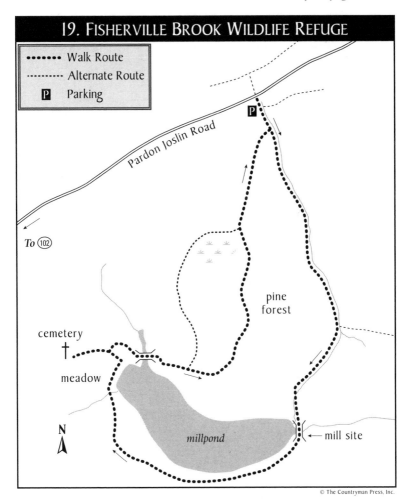

19. FISHERVILLE BROOK WILDLIFE REFUGE

•••••• Walk Route
---------- Alternate Route
P Parking

Pardon Joslin Road

P

To (102)

pine forest

cemetery †

meadow

N

millpond

mill site

© The Countryman Press, Inc.

Trail

Take a moment to look over the kiosk and perhaps pick up a trail map. A trail blazed in orange begins to the left of the kiosk, but for this walk take the trail blazed in blue and orange that runs just to the right of the kiosk. Immediately, you pass another blue trail on the right; it will be your return route.

A bridge on the Fisherville Brook Refuge trail.

The trail, an old lane in this area, is smooth and easy to walk. Most of the way it is carpeted with pine needles because it runs below some of the tallest pines in the area. There are also places where vigorous young pines are growing beneath the old matriarchs.

As you pass a wet area on the left, the lane splits, the orange blazes going left. That path eventually circles back to the parking lot. Instead, take the blue-blazed right fork. You quickly reach the millpond, a lovely little lake of turtles, frogs, and often ducks and other birds. We have seen flocks of showy hooded mergansers here in spring, and there are usually kingfishers, orioles, and swallows here in summer.

A bridge crosses the old dam spillway, enabling you to see some of the vanished mill's stonework where the water cascades from the pond into a brook. Once, this spot might have been the center of the area's activity. Now, it is quiet, peaceful, and contemplative.

(From here, the brook flows a few miles south to Fisherville, once a thriving little mill village. Now, the entire village is gone except for stone foundations.)

After crossing the bridge, the path curves to the right, circling the pond. For most of this stretch the path runs through dense bushes, and the water is not always visible. However, after crossing a tiny brook (elevated walkways carry you over damp spots), the path emerges in the first of the open meadows. Stone walls and treed borders surround the grassy areas, and you may see more wildlife here, perhaps bluebirds, but more likely swallows. Numerous birdhouses are nailed to the trees and to posts in the fields. We've also seen deer in these fields.

The path skirts the right edge of the field, following the shoreline of the pond, which is now easily seen through a thin screen of trees. Far to the left, at the top of a hill, you can see a few homes and other buildings.

When you reach a stone wall, the path curves left for a short distance, then goes through an opening in the wall and enters a second field. Before entering this field, however, you can take a detour path to the left to a small cemetery that is interesting because it was built above the surrounding ground level.

When you return to the blue trail, you'll find it only edges the second field briefly, quickly returning to forest and crossing a stream that feeds the pond. Wood ducks sometimes can be found here, and beavers frequently use the brook. You may see stumps of trees they have cut or their gnawing on trunks. This is an excellent place to linger. It is your last view of the pond.

From the bridge, the trail runs through an idyllic grove of tall pines with little underbrush. The chief residents here seem to be red squirrels. Even when they are not seen or heard, their presence is readily noticed by the piles of pinecone remnants at the base of favorite trees or around rocks they use as tables.

You'll see a side trail, blazed in yellow, breaking off to the left. That path circles a small swampy area before rejoining the blue trail. Both trails go over small ridges and weave among the pines as they zigzag through the forest. In minutes—too quickly for most walkers—you are back on the lane you began on, just a few steps from your car.

20 · Wickaboxet

Walking distance: 2½ miles
Walking time: 2 hours

Not many walkers visit the Wickaboxet Wildlife Management Area these days. Those who don't know it are missing a good thing.

Wickaboxet, a mid-sized management area at 679 acres, is in West Greenwich, just south of the Coventry line. It was the first state forest and once was extensively used for picnics and other outdoor recreation, but in recent years it has been overshadowed by the much larger Arcadia Management Area a few miles south.

Hunters use the place in autumn, occasionally horseback riders use the old roads, and young people sometimes climb the area's featured attraction, Rattlesnake Ledge. But for the most part Wickaboxet, ever since a devastating fire in the 1950s, has been left to the squirrels, deer, and songbirds—and to the resurgent trees, which are again thriving and making the forest more attractive each year.

There are no marked hiking trails. Instead, you follow the woods roads. The 2½-mile route described here runs along two sides of the state property and cuts through the interior, finishing with a climactic climb up Rattlesnake Ledge. No, you aren't likely to find any rattlesnakes; they've been gone for decades.

The more ambitious can walk much farther by staying on the perimeter road, but it eventually runs off state property and you will have to retrace your steps.

Access

To reach the entrance to Wickaboxet, drive RI 102 in West Greenwich to Plain Meeting House Road, then go west for 3 miles. A sign and a small parking area are on the right side of the road.

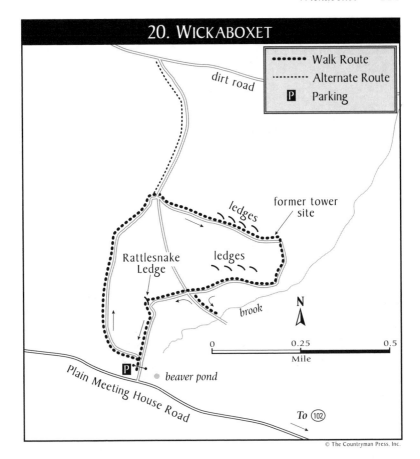

20. WICKABOXET

Walk Route
Alternate Route
Parking

dirt road

ledges

former tower site

ledges

Rattlesnake Ledge

brook

N

0   0.25   0.5
Mile

P   beaver pond

Plain Meeting House Road

To (102)

© The Countryman Press, Inc.

Trail

Before beginning your walk, take a few minutes to look over a beaver pond. A short lane off the paved road just before the parking lot will take you to the beavers' dam at a culvert. Even if you don't see any beavers, knowing they are close by can put you in the right mood for this walk.

The entrance road is gated just beyond the parking area and forks almost immediately beyond the gate. Inside the fork, hidden in brush, is a small cellar hole, a reminder that this place once was farmland.

Massive Rattlesnake Ledge invites exploration.

Unless you are interested only in Rattlesnake Ledge, take the left fork. It is an easy, open lane that runs slightly uphill as it curves to the right. Immediately, you will notice hundreds of young pine trees flanking the road. They were planted several years ago to hasten reforestation after one of the worst forest fires in Rhode Island history hit this area. Now, virtually all scars of the fire are gone. Through much of this walk you will see pines of various ages and sizes. Some were planted shortly after the fire, others were added much later, and some are natural offspring. The hardwoods, too, especially the oaks, are doing well and add good color, particularly in fall.

Birds abound. In the deeper woods, you are likely to see flycatchers, woodpeckers, chickadees, thrushes, and warblers. You also may see, depending somewhat on the season, waxwings, thrashers, towhees, and grosbeaks. There will be squirrels and chipmunks along the trail as well, and occasionally you may come upon a grouse dusting itself in the lane. Deer and coyotes frequently use this road, so you can expect to see their tracks and/or scat.

Before you have gone 1 mile, your road will merge with another one coming in from the right. You can continue straight ahead for more views of surging forest, but eventually you'll have to return because the road runs off state property. For this walk, turn to the right, and then turn left at another fork soon after. You will again be on a path flanked by young pines. Soon, though, the lane opens a bit and you will be able to see low stone ledges off to the left. At the end of a rocky ridge is a side trail that curls uphill to the left. Take it. It goes only a few yards to the top of the ridge, where a fire tower once stood. All that remain are a few concrete anchors.

After this brief detour, resume following the road as it swings downhill, curving below another section of ledges, now almost obscured by pines. In about ½ mile from the tower site you reach a crossroad. A detour on the narrow path going left takes you to a small brook that is lovely in spring. While walking this path once, I was rewarded with the sighting of a large deer that leaped up and bounded through the forest, flashing its white flag of a tail.

Back on the main road, just beyond the crossroad, begin looking into the woods on the right for Wickaboxet's famed Rattlesnake Ledge. Not far off the road and looming high above the surroundings, it is a massive rock outcropping that demands inspection. The most prominent path goes up and around the left end of the ridge. While you are not likely to find rattlesnakes, be careful anyway in climbing the ledge. A fall could be just as big a problem as a snakebite.

The view from the top is simply delightful—and surprising after previously walking on relatively level terrain. You can see for miles over the treetops; in fact, your view is of what appears to be unbroken forest. Take your time and enjoy the view. Walk the length of the ridge. Linger awhile.

When you're able to tear yourself away, return to the base of the ledge and walk along it for another perspective. It is quite a cliff.

Getting back to your car from the ledge is a matter of simply going back out to the dirt road, turning right, and walking ¼ mile or so.

21 · Carbuncle Pond–Moosup River

Walking distance: 3 miles
Walking time: 1½ to 2 hours

Carbuncle Pond, almost on the Connecticut line in Coventry, is a clean, deep pond that boasts some of the best fishing in the area. The Moosup River, which runs nearby, is clean, fast, and shallow. Both are great places for walkers to visit.

The entire pond and most of the adjoining area are part of the state's 1,500-acre Nicholas Farm Wildlife Management Area. However, the western shoreline of Carbuncle is private property, so a full circuit of the pond is not permitted.

Years ago the pond was popular locally for swimming and family outings, but when beavers dammed an outlet stream, the water level rose and flooded the road that led to a sandy beach. Now, although the road still provides access to the pond, and it is still popular with fishermen, few others come here, except for hunters in fall and early winter.

On this 3-mile route, you not only follow the pond's shoreline to a marsh, but you also will get a look at a small beaver pond, its dam, and lodge and can detour to an old railroad trestle that hangs high above the Moosup River. The route then returns through a tranquil pine forest, dips down to a scenic little waterfall on the river, then meanders through woods and fields back to the pond. The beginning and end of this route are not marked but walkers will follow the blue-blazed North South Trail (NST) through the middle segment.

Access

Drive RI 14 or RI 117 into western Coventry. The two highways merge just east of the Moosup River. From this junction, continue west for 1 mile

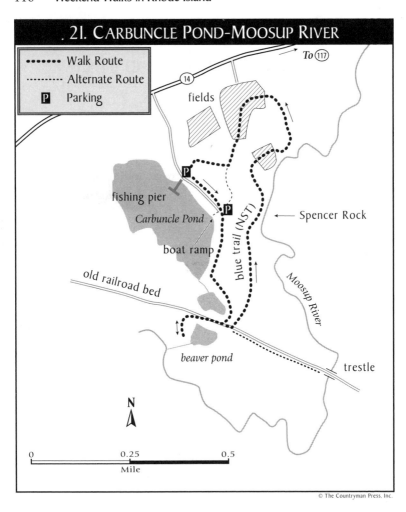

21. Carbuncle Pond–Moosup River

••••••• Walk Route
---------- Alternate Route
P Parking

To (117)

(14)

fields

fishing pier

Carbuncle Pond

boat ramp

P

P

Spencer Rock

blue trail (NST)

old railroad bed

beaver pond

Moosup River

trestle

N

0   0.25   0.5
Mile

© The Countryman Press, Inc.

and look for a sign for the Carbuncle Pond Fishing Area on the left. Follow the narrow dirt entrance road until reaching the pond. There are several parking areas along the pond but, for this walk, park in the lot near a long fishing pier that reaches out into the water.

Trail

Begin by following the sandy entrance road until its end in another large parking area where there is a boat ramp. Now take a footpath that runs along the shore to what used to be the beach area. A guardrail remains. This spot offers good views of the pond. Several paths run into the woods. Ignore them and walk to the far end of the guardrail, then take an open lane that runs directly away from the pond. It parallels a marsh where waterfowl, swallows, and frogs can often be found, along with the occasional otter or muskrat and, in early summer, thousands of water lilies.

In a matter of minutes you emerge on a high ridge that once was a railroad bed. Walk the ridge to the right. There is water on both sides, the marsh on your right and a small pond created by beavers on the left. The best views of both are about halfway across the water. At present, a beaver lodge stands across the narrow pond on your left. The dam is at the far end of the pond; if you want a closer look, stay on the old railroad bed until you are past the water, then take a path down to the left. This dam has been here for many years and many generations of beavers. It is worth the extra steps.

When you're ready to resume walking, climb back up to the railroad bed and return, now going right. Go past the lane that you took along the marsh. In just a few more steps is a second lane heading north into a pine forest. This one carries the blue blazes of the NST. For this walk, turn left here. But those who want a little more distance and a look at the high trestle over the river can continue following the railroad bed southeast. It's just over ½ mile to the trestle and back. The bridge, built on a foundation of huge stone blocks, now has a chainlink fence along both sides to protect walkers. It would be a long drop into the river.

Back at the blue-blazed lane going north into the pines, you'll find a pleasant, quiet segment. You will pass many side trails; stay with the blue blazes until reaching a small open field. The blue blazes run across this field, then curve around to the right and return to the river. For those wanting a shortcut, look for a short path to the right and a steep, eroded

Carbuncle Pond remains popular with fishermen.

slope just as you reach the open field. Both routes will take you to the waterfall, a lovely spot known as Spencer Rock. Here, where water roars over the smooth rock shelves in early spring and gurgles gently in summer, is a great place to linger. It is roughly the halfway point in this walk.

Numerous trails lead away from Spencer Rock, including some that would take you fairly directly back to Carbuncle Pond, but for this walk continue following the NST markers as they follow the river briefly, then go through a grove of pines. The trail emerges into a field but goes along its right edge and quickly returns to forest.

When the blue trail reaches an old farm lane, you have another chance for a shortcut. Taking the lane left will enable you to reach the return road quickly. However, the blue blazes go right and within moments the trail takes you into a hayfield. There is no worn path across this field but if you look at the far left corner of the field you can see a blue-painted post. That is your target. Like many open fields, this one may contain foxes or hawks, and in snow you are likely to find many tracks.

At the far side of the field, you are again close to the river, but the trail turns away from the water, going left into a spectacular pine forest. Many of the trees are huge but the trail itself is lined with thousands of vigorous young trees. There is some up-and-down going here, but this is a lovely segment indeed.

This time, when you emerge into a field, forget the blue blazes. They go to the right to the paved road, Route 14, that you drove earlier, and then head north. Instead, follow the tree line on your left to a farm lane that cuts through the large field. Crossing this field (to the left) in spring or summer adds a feeling of venturing into a prairie. Butterflies, dragonflies, swallows, and wildflowers are your companions.

When this road returns to trees, you can see the shortcut lane on the left and an entrance lane into another large field on your right. Birds and animal tracks are likely in both places. But stay on the main road as it goes through a sandy area. When it makes a 90-degree turn to the left, look for a faint path angling to the right. This is the trickiest spot on the entire walk. You want to find a tractor entrance where the thin line of trees on your right meets the woods straight ahead.

If you can't find this opening, return to the main road. It will lead you to the second parking lot.

If you do find the opening next to the woods, take it only about 20 yards, then look for a narrow path entering the forest on your left. Follow this path and it will lead you directly into the big parking lot by the fishing pier and your car.

22 · Parker Woodland

Walking distance: 4 miles
Walking time: 2½ to 3 hours

A walk through the George B. Parker Woodland in Coventry is a stroll through history. It enables you to take a look at the Rhode Island of two hundred and three hundred years ago in the stone remains of mills, farmhouses, roads, and fences. And it visits mysterious stone cairns that may be much older than three hundred years.

Years ago, the land now called Parker Woodland was considered a lively, and deadly, place. Two taverns that stood along Maple Valley Road, now the access route to the refuge, were known for the ruffians they attracted and tales of shootings punctuate the region's history and lore. Local residents used to speak of troubled spirits roaming the older homes. Now, Parker Woodland is extremely quiet, almost eerie, with its many reminders of the past silently reposing among the stately trees, surging undergrowth, and timeless boulders.

This trail is in the Coventry Tract of Parker, a large property owned by the Audubon Society of Rhode Island. The refuge also spills over into Foster. The route described here includes part of a short trail that links the two tracts, so walkers can easily extend their visit. This walk also can be shortened at several points, but doing this entire 4-mile route is recommended because each shortcut eliminates important features.

Adding a loop in the Foster tract would make a hike of about 7 miles. That trail has its own stonework—a quarry site and more cellar holes—but probably does not equal the Coventry loop in interesting features.

Because this is an Audubon Society refuge, where no hunting is allowed, it is a great place to visit in autumn and early winter when the

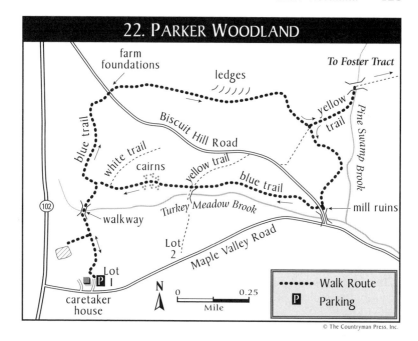

abundance of hunters can make walking in state management properties uncomfortable.

Access

To reach the Coventry Tract, turn east from RI 102 onto Maple Valley Road. The first house on the left is the home of the refuge's caretaker. Just beyond is a large parking area labeled Lot No. 1. Begin your walk from this lot. A second parking lot farther down Maple Valley Road is rarely open these days.

Trail

The trail from Lot 1 begins behind a large kiosk that usually features Audubon Society news and wildlife information, as well as maps and pamphlets pertaining to Parker. The path, blazed here in orange, runs immediately into forest and soon follows the first of many stone walls you'll see on this walk.

At the first trail junction, the orange trail turns to the right, climbing over a stone wall on a wooden walkway. However, first take a few moments to walk to the left. This unblazed path quickly emerges at the edge of an open field where, in spring or summer, you may see bluebirds or swallows using birdhouses or hawks soaring above. It's a brief detour but often worth the extra steps.

Back on the orange trail, cross the stone wall and in moments you reach another raised walkway, this one a long, curving structure that enables you to cross a brook and swampy area. Go slowly; the water attracts much wildlife, from songbirds and frogs to salamanders and wildflowers.

Just beyond the walkway, the trail climbs onto higher, rockier ground and meets the blue loop trail. This junction is less than ½ mile from your start. You can go either way on the blue trail, of course, but for this walk go left. The trail runs slightly uphill through a vibrant, mixed forest and the walking is fairly easy. On all sides, scattered through the woods, are boulders of all sizes, showing how difficult it must have been to farm this land.

Shortly after you start seeing more stone walls, the trail runs beside a low stone rectangle that was the foundation of a building, believed to be a barn, and in a few more steps you reach an old road flanked on both sides by stone walls. This is Biscuit Hill Road, a legendary passage supposedly named because during the American Revolution a wagon loaded with biscuits meant for Rochambeau's army was spilled here. You could shorten your walk by taking the old road and white blazes to the right. It is an extremely attractive lane and would take you down to the brook, the old mill site, and another crossing of the blue trail. But you would be missing some of the area's man-made and natural highlights, so instead, follow the blue trail directly across the road to the Vaughn farm site, just under 1 mile from your start.

A sign beside a large cellar hole identifies this spot as the former home of Captain Caleb Vaughn, and the sign also provides substantial background on the farm, although at this writing the sign is faded and difficult

Who built the stone cairns at Parker? Nobody knows.

to read. This is a good place to linger, to examine the workmanship of the cellar and the stone-lined well, and perhaps to contemplate what life here may have been like so many years ago.

The trail continues through the "back yard" of the farmhouse, running through a grove of vigorous young pines, then through an extremely rocky area. You will work your way around and over ledges, some of which, legends say, formerly sheltered rattlesnakes and bobcats. For almost 1 mile after leaving the farm site, you weave through this rocky area. You will cross one woods lane that provides another shortcut possibility, to the right, but you are better off staying with the blue blazes.

When you reach a yellow-blazed cross trail, beside an immense boulder, take a brief detour. The yellow trail, to the left, is the connector to the refuge's Foster Tract but it is worth walking because it runs through a spectacular little ravine beside a brook. This is Pine Swamp Brook, and the yellow trail follows it upstream, advancing along a series of falls and pools while climbing down and past rugged ledges. Take this trail as far as a bridge over the brook, another great place to rest and marvel.

When ready to resume your walk, retrace the yellow trail back to the blue trail and turn left. (The yellow trail could be taken as another shortcut but it misses the mill ruins.) The blue trail curls down near Pine Swamp Brook again, then up through the forest and emerges once more on Biscuit Hill Road at about 2¾ miles. Just to your left, off the left side of the road, are the impressive stone remains of a sawmill and the stone-lined hole where the water wheel stood. Also lying in the woods are the foundations of other buildings that were part of the mill complex. Portions of what was a sluiceway can be seen on both sides of the road, and off to the right is a stream and a section of a dam that held the water for the mill. Now, this stream, Turkey Meadow Brook, is a lively little stream running over thousands of rocks. This is yet another great place to linger.

There is more history, and much more mystery, still ahead. The blue trail follows Turkey Meadow Brook upstream, running along a ridge well above the water. In just under ½ mile from the old mill site you will again reach the yellow shortcut trail at a bridge. The path across this bridge would take you to parking Lot No. 2. Instead, remain on the blue trail, following the brook, and in a few minutes you will reach what many people consider the most intriguing area of Parker Woodland: the stone cairns.

The cairns—cone-shaped mounds of stone—defy explanation. Archaeologists have studied many areas of Parker but they have not determined who built the dozens of cairns, or when, or why. Perhaps it is better this way; now each visitor can speculate on their origin. Were they built by American Indians for some religious ritual? Did some pre-Columbian explorers use them to mark their way by the stars? Or were they simply the work of some fussy farmer who wasn't satisfied with throwing the rocks onto a pile?

Take time to look over the cairns and note their workmanship. Some have tumbled but others are filled with stones so meticulously fitted together they are still solid after two or three centuries or more. Restrict your study to looking, however; the Audubon Society allows no disturbing of the cairns.

The cairns are a fitting climax to your visit to Parker. From the cairns it is a short walk through a magnificent grove of beeches and another area of imposing boulders back to the orange trail. All that remains, then, is a left turn for the return across the boardwalks to your car—and much to think about.

23 · Barden Reservoir

Walking distance: 4 miles
Walking time: 2 hours

This is among my favorite places to walk. It's a stroll in the country. Here you see lots of water and woods along with some farms, usually plenty of wildlife, a high man-made waterfall, and several reminders of the area's past.

Barden Reservoir is a pond in Foster and Scituate that is part of the huge Scituate Reservoir system. As such, it and the land that surrounds it are off-limits to the public, but roads that traverse the area provide easy and pleasant access. This walk is entirely on these little-used country roads, most of them unpaved. In this loop of just over 4 miles, walkers will pass only half a dozen houses and are not likely to be passed by even that many cars.

Because the walk is on the roads, it can be done when deep snow, excessive mud, or intense heat makes woods walking difficult. However, the best times may be in spring and early summer when birdlife is most active. Many waterfowl stop by during migration, and numerous songbirds nest along the route.

Access

Drive RI 102 in western Scituate and turn west onto Central Pike. In 1.6 miles, you cross into Foster and reach a bridge. You should drive across the bridge and park on the opposite side, where there is more room.

Trail

I recommend beginning this loop by going west. That gets most of the uphill walking out of the way early and saves the route's highlights for the second half of the trip.

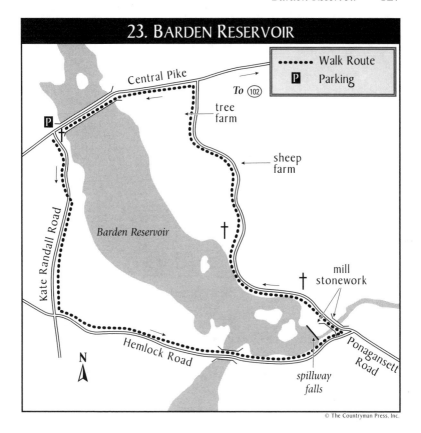

23. BARDEN RESERVOIR

Central Pike

••••••• Walk Route

P Parking

To (102)

tree farm

sheep farm

Kate Randall Road

Barden Reservoir

mill stonework

Hemlock Road

Ponagansett Road

N

spillway falls

© The Countryman Press, Inc.

Before walking, however, take a moment to look over the ponds on each side of the bridge. With their clear water, pine-covered shores, and unmarred islands, they appear transplanted from some wilderness setting of perhaps Maine or New Hampshire.

Also take a look at a small graveyard on a knoll just beyond the bridge on the left. Most of the stones date from the mid-1800s and the dominant name is Randall, a family name you'll soon see again.

Just up Central Pike from the bridge, turn left on Kate Randall Road. This gravel and dirt road runs mostly uphill. For much of this section, mixed woods accented with stone walls are on both sides. Many of the

Forested islands are part of the view at Barden.

walls are on reservoir property, showing that this was farmland before acquired by the state for the water project.

Although there are a few homes on this road, there is so little traffic that I once came across a grouse taking a dust bath in the middle of the road at midday.

At the next crossroads, 1 mile from your start, turn left onto another gravel road called Hemlock Road. Now you will be going downhill. Soon you'll reach a lovely area with tall trees and ledges, particularly on the left. Trees and ferns grow out of crevices in the rocks, and many boulders are coated with moss and lichens. Little evergreen plants called ground pine carpet the forest floor.

You cross a narrow bridge, where swallows are often abundant in summer, before reaching a paved portion of the road. A short distance ahead is the reservoir's dam, an inviting place to linger. This spot provides good views of the pond, the earthen dam, and the spillway—which sends water cascading into a deep gorge. At this point, you are about halfway through your walk.

For another, and perhaps better, perspective of the gorge and falls, continue walking downhill a hundred yards or so to the next intersection and turn left onto Ponagansett Road. You'll quickly reach a bridge, where you may want to linger again.

Not only can you see the spillway falls, but below you is a rushing stream and the remnants of mill stonework. Several mills stood here, at different times, in the prereservoir days, and parts of dams, sluices, bridges, and foundations can be seen on both sides of the existing bridge. More mill relics are just up the road, including a stone-lined raceway that can be seen on both sides of your road.

You pass a well-kept cemetery—Barden is one of the prominent names—and then the road, gravel once more, runs close to the water for some distance. This is a lovely stretch. Swallows swoop over the water. Orioles nest above the road. Thrushes sing in the forest. I've also seen wild turkeys, otters, coyotes, and deer while walking this section.

Soon, though, the road curves away from the pond and climbs uphill. You pass another cemetery, small, weathered, and very old, on the left and some majestic hickory trees, then reach a farm where you usually can see sheep in the fields. I've seen deer in these pastures as well. After the road makes a bend to the right, you pass a tree farm on the left.

At the next intersection, you have returned to Central Pike. Turn left and walk the ½ mile to the bridge and your car.

24 · Sprague Farm

Walking distance: 4 miles
Walking time: 2 to 2½ hours

Sprague Farm is a town-owned property in Glocester that keeps growing in both size and stature. Recent additions have boosted the area to about 1,000 acres, and it has begun attracting more and more walkers.

There is much to see here. Even though there are few trails at present, walkers will get a good look at a thriving forest, some open fields, and numerous reminders of the past in stone walls, stone bridges, and several cellar holes left over from abandoned homes.

Sprague Farm also has considerable wildlife. Deer are common, both in the woods and in the fields, and walkers have seen signs of fox, coyote, fisher, and raccoon. Birds ranging from songbirds to grouse, hawks, and owls frequent the property, and in summer and fall the open meadows attract many butterflies, bumblebees, and dragonflies.

The property has its share of unique creatures. It is said to be the only place in Rhode Island where the black-throated blue warbler nests, and the huge pileated woodpeckers have been seen here. The forest includes a cedar swamp while the upland area features striped maple, a species not widespread in Rhode Island.

Most of the walking is along old roads. The 4-mile route described here extends from the main loop trail to an interesting old homestead site and back. Those wanting a shorter walk can do only the main loop, a distance of about 3 miles, or go partway around the loop, then go out to a paved road and return to the parking lot, a distance of slightly over 2 miles.

Visitors should keep in mind that Sprague Farm is reserved for hunters in November and December.

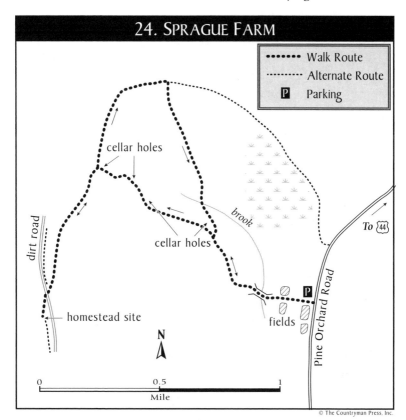

24. SPRAGUE FARM

•••••• Walk Route
············ Alternate Route
P Parking

cellar holes

dirt road

cellar holes

brook

To {44}

homestead site

fields

Pine Orchard Road

N

0   0.5   1
Mile

© The Countryman Press, Inc.

Access

Drive US 44 west 2 miles from the traffic light in the village of Chepachet to Pine Orchard Road and turn left. In slightly under 1 mile you will reach a parking lot and sign on the right. You will pass another sign for Sprague Farm and a narrow trail on the right before reaching the parking lot for this hike.

Trail

Before starting on the loop trail, marked with a sign, look over the open fields along Pine Orchard Road. At dawn and dusk these fields attract deer,

Forest has reclaimed most of Sprague Farm.

and when the goldenrods and other wildflowers are in bloom they draw butterflies and other insects.

Soon after beginning the trail, which here runs between stone walls, you reach two more open meadows, one on each side of the trail. These, too, are worth spending a few minutes to explore.

Beyond the meadows the trail runs beneath tall pines and hemlocks, and you quickly reach the first stone bridge. In about ⅓ mile you reach a fork; an arrow suggests you remain on the open road, the left fork. You will return on the other branch.

Just beyond this fork are stone foundations that invite inspection. One on the left side of the trail was probably for livestock. To the right of the trail is a cellar with a huge stone base for a fireplace. Growing out of the cellar is a towering pine, an indicator of how long ago this house was abandoned.

After the trail curves to the right you will see a second cellar, also on the right. This one has collapsed more than the first one and might be even older, judging from the trees growing in and around it.

Still more cellars are ahead. After crossing a second stone bridge in a grove of hemlocks, begin looking on the right for a big cellar, considerably larger than those you have passed. It is about 1 mile from your start and across from a lane that joins your road from the left. This cellar, and the other stonework nearby, also should be inspected, not just walked past.

From this spot, walkers seeking a shorter route should follow arrows on trees and continue straight ahead on the road. If, however, you want to do the entire 4 miles and see more intriguing features, turn left at the junction, marked presently with blue paint.

This left lane crosses a brook then runs through dense young forest where, in snow, I've found tracks of snowshoe hares. When you reach another woods road, turn left, then look into the forest on the right. There you will find another large cellar, but what might be more interesting is the other stonework. Just to the right of the cellar is a sign indicating a historical cemetery. However, the upright stones behind the sign suggest they once held up a farm building, probably a granary. I have not found a cemetery and wonder if somebody mistook the granary stones for tombstones.

You could continue walking this road in either direction, but at some point you'll have to turn around and return up the lane you walked a few minutes earlier to the junction with the large cellar in order to make your way back to your car. After backtracking to that junction, rejoin the main loop trail by turning left.

This next section of about ½ mile is picturesque in all seasons with tall trees, a healthy sprinkling of mountain laurel, and scattered boulders. It is a mostly downhill route, and shortly after crossing still another stone bridge the arrows will point toward a narrower path going to the right. If you want to cut the walk short, you can continue on the old road. It will take you past the cedar swamp out to Pine Orchard Road. However, that stretch is often wet (nearly impassable in early spring), so taking the interior path is recommended.

This path curves often as it runs through thickets of laurel and pine groves. You again have to cross a brook and at present the bridge is a couple of planks since the old stone slabs were displaced, perhaps by a spring freshet. From the brook to the point where the path rejoins the main trail is a short distance. Then, turn left on the main trail and return to the parking lot.

25 · Durfee Hill

Walking distance: 3 miles
Walking time: 2 hours

The Durfee Hill Wildlife Management Area is a state-owned property of more than 1,200 acres in Glocester but it is somewhat disjointed, split by roads and sections of private property. The largest contiguous segment is a short distance east of the area chosen for this walk, but this area was picked because it offers several of Durfee Hill's top attractions in terms of scenery, terrain, and wildlife.

This walk is relatively short—just under 3 miles—but it includes two loops plus a high, imposing rock wall, two ponds, pine and hemlock groves, a marsh, open fields, a well-kept graveyard hidden in the forest, and enough up-and-down going to provide a workout.

In addition, there is always the possibility of seeing deer, beavers, coyotes, red squirrels, wood ducks, herons, wild turkeys, grouse, and many kinds of songbirds along this route.

Keep in mind, however, that there are no blazes along these paths; some care must be taken to stay on the route outlined here and not to wander off onto side trails, many of which run off state land. You can easily shorten the hike by choosing to walk only one of the loops since they are divided by the highway on which you will be parked.

Also remember that Durfee teems with hunters in November and December. Therefore, early autumn, late winter, and spring might be better times to explore these trails. In summer, the dense conifers and ponds attract more mosquitoes than most hikers will want to fight.

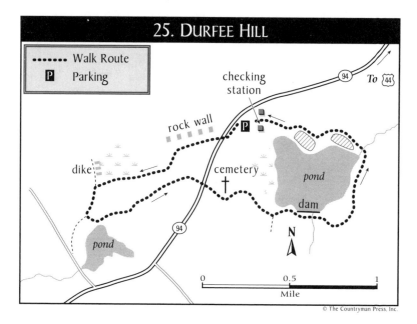

25. DURFEE HILL

••••••• Walk Route

P Parking

checking station

To (44)

(94)

rock wall

dike

cemetery

pond

dam

(94)

pond

N

0   0.5   1
Mile

© The Countryman Press, Inc.

Access

To reach the start, drive US 44 in Glocester almost to the Connecticut line, turning south on RI 94 (Reynolds Road) across from Bowdish Reservoir. Follow RI 94 1.3 miles to a parking area beside a hunter checking station, on the left. Signs indicate this is the Durfee Hill Management Area.

Trail

Before walking, take a moment to look over the surrounding countryside. Below and to the right of the parking lot, as you face the checking station building, lies a shallow pond. In summer, it is decorated with water lilies and usually has swallows swooping above it. In spring and fall, the field in the foreground and the high, forested ridge on the far side of the pond add more color. In winter, the combination of snow and the deep green hemlocks produces an idyllic scene whether the pond is open, locked in ice, or covered with snow.

You will conclude your walk with a circuit of this pond, but begin by walking up the roadway, RI 94, to the left as you leave the parking lot. The part of the management area that includes the high ledges is on the opposite side of the road. Stay on the paved road only about ¼ mile until reaching a path on your right between utility poles numbered 33 and 33½. As with other trails here, this is an unmarked path and is relatively narrow at its start.

Almost immediately, you can see the high rock wall looming through the pine trees on the right. This is the highest of several cliffs in the area and occasionally you will see climbers here practicing their techniques. The wall invites inspection.

The path runs parallel to the wall for about ¼ mile. There is a side path that enables you to go on top of the ledge if so desired. Where the wall begins to flatten, your entrance path curves to the left and joins a wider lane. Take this lane to the right. Now you are walking among taller pines and the lane is often carpeted with pine needles.

The lane winds downhill and then runs along the edge of a brushy marsh, which often attracts swallows, kingbirds, warblers, and other songbirds. When you reach an open area you can go a few steps to the right, onto an earthen dike that helped create the marsh, for a good look at the marsh and its inhabitants, both birds and plants.

A trail runs across the dike and into the forest beyond, but for this walk, return to the main lane. It soon curves left, away from the marsh. This is an easy, open, downhill segment. Again, ignore side trails; most were made by motorcyclists.

When the lane reaches a Y-junction, turn to the left. (Going right will quickly take you out of the forest and onto a road). By going to the left, you will be walking parallel to the shore of a small pond. Unfortunately, there is little access to the shore itself. This segment is one of the tricky spots on this walk. The main trail, worn by all-terrain vehicles, continues circling the pond and soon runs off state property. Instead, just beyond an extremely muddy area, look on the left for a fainter trail going up a very steep hill in the pines. Take this path. (If you're unable to find this path, stay on the main trail out of the woods; you can then walk the highway back to where you need to be.)

The steep trail goes up and over a ridge, then ends at a larger lane. Turn left. This lane soon passes a large rock outcropping on the right. It is not as high as the rock wall you passed earlier but still worth a look. Shortly beyond the outcropping, the trail dips through a hemlock stand and reaches still another lane, part of the lane you walked earlier. This time, turn to the right. In minutes, you will emerge (behind a guardrail) onto RI 94.

You could simply walk the highway to the left back to your car, but you have gone less than $1\frac{1}{2}$ miles. Instead, almost directly across the road you'll see an orange-barred lane, beside pole 35. Take this lane into the forest. In moments you will see a cemetery, just to the left of the trail, surrounded by a stone wall, an iron gate, and tall pines. Clean and clipped, this graveyard dates back to the 1820s.

Beyond the graveyard, the going again gets a little tricky, with several side paths that can be confusing. It is best to stay on the main lane as it curves left just beyond the cemetery, running downhill, and then goes right and enters an open, sandy area. The lane ends in the open area, but if you walk the right edge of the clearing you will find a path that leads downhill, to the left, back into forest. This trail quickly reaches a T-junction; go left.

Now you are on a lane that runs along a brook. In minutes, you will reach an earthen dam and the large pond you saw earlier from the parking lot. This spot provides great views of the water, the wood duck houses to the right, the water lilies (in season), and the fields across the way. Look also at the brook below the dam; chewed saplings and sticks show beavers sometimes travel through here. In fact, beavers periodically dam up the culvert between the pond and brook.

Again, you can shorten the walk by walking the left (west) shore of the pond back to your car, but that area tends to be wet, and you would miss some of the finest sections of forest as well as close-up looks at the fields and old fruit trees that attract wildlife on the far side of the pond.

High rock wall is just off the road at Durfee Hill.

So cross the dam, to the right. Sighting down the right (east) shore you may see a beaver lodge in the corner of the pond. The trail, however, goes uphill, away from the water. Soon you begin a long, sweeping curve to the left, and this is your longest climb of the day. When the path levels out, you are atop a ridge in a grove of hemlocks, some of which are of magnificent sizes and shapes.

You are circling the pond but for most of this section you cannot see the water because of the dense foliage. The trail is easy to follow—it runs the crest of the ridge—and ignore all paths that run off to either side.

The descent is gradual, with some up-and-down, but easy and pleasant. Shortly after you begin seeing the pond again through trees on the left, the trail crosses a pretty little brook on a plank bridge and ends at an open field. Look over this field and those ahead carefully; I've seen deer here more than once. Sometimes these fields are planted in grain for the wildlife.

A tractor lane runs along the right edge of the fields. Take it. It meanders past the fields, small woodlots, old apple trees, and meadows all the way up to the parking lot at the hunter checking station. But don't be in a hurry to finish; this final segment is likely to be filled with wildflowers and butterflies in spring and fall, dragonflies in summer, and birds at all times. And there's always that chance of seeing a fox or deer.

26 • Walkabout Trail

Walking distance: 8 miles
Walking time: 4 hours

The Walkabout Trail is one of the old favorites of hikers in the northern part of Rhode Island, and it remains popular because it is still a delight. It offers not only a variety of features but also three loops that can make the walk as short as 2 miles or as long as 8 miles. The third loop is 6 miles.

All the loops begin and end together, near a beach on Bowdish Reservoir in the George Washington Management Area in Glocester. All offer good views of the reservoir and run along the edge of a campground. The longer trails ramble through dense woodlands and past another pond. The widest circuit, the 8-mile loop described here, also goes through a portion of adjacent Pulaski Park (see Walk 27), running briefly on a cross-country ski trail, then circles through an impressive hemlock grove and visits an interesting wildlife marsh.

Most of the trail is relatively flat but there are numerous areas of rocky footing that will require some care, and in a few places the path crosses low-lying areas that are likely to be muddy in wet periods. The trail is usually well maintained and there are numerous wooden walkways over boggy spots and some trash barrels where the path crosses gravel roads. Early autumn, just after most of the campers have departed, is probably the best time to do this hike. From mid-October to the end of February, hikers are required to wear orange hats or vests, as they are on all state management areas in hunting season.

The Walkabout was cut and named by Australian sailors back in 1965, while their ship, the *Perth*, was in dry dock in Newport. The name refers to the wanderings of the Australian aborigines.

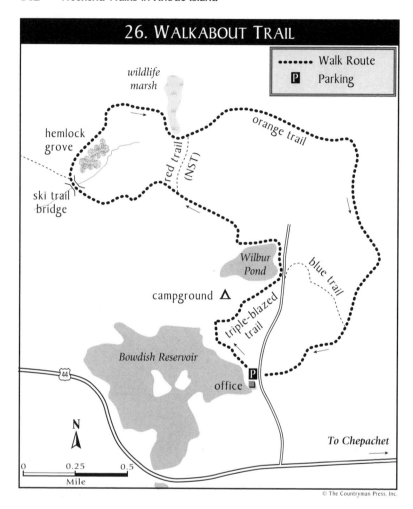

26. WALKABOUT TRAIL

•••••• Walk Route

P Parking

wildlife marsh

hemlock grove

orange trail

red trail (NST)

ski trail bridge

Wilbur Pond

blue trail

campground ▲

triple-blazed trail

Bowdish Reservoir

44

office

N

To Chepachet

0   0.25   0.5
Mile

© The Countryman Press, Inc.

Access

To reach the trailhead, take US 44 to George Washington Camping Area, about 4.5 miles west of Chepachet. Turn right onto the campground road and continue 0.3 mile until you reach a lane that runs to the left by a park building. Turn and park along this wide lane. Entry into the park requires a fee during the summer months.

Trail

All three loops of the Walkabout Trail begin just to the right of the reservoir beach. The 8-mile loop is blazed in orange, the 6-mile loop in red, and the 2-mile loop in blue. A fourth blaze was recently added; it refers to the North South Trail (NST) that runs through this area on its way from Rhode Island's southern coast to the Massachusetts line. Through the early going, trees carry all four blazes.

You begin by following the reservoir shoreline, walking through a dense but pleasant forest of mountain laurel, pines, and hemlocks. The path weaves among boulders and there are several cutoffs to rocky points jutting out into the water. The footing is rocky, though, and exposed roots can trip you up, so pay some attention to what is at your feet.

In less than $\frac{1}{2}$ mile, the trail swings to the right and runs along the edge of the camping area, several times edging the rear of campsites. Soon, you are walking on a woods lane and where this lane joins a larger gravel road, the trail splits. The blue blazes go out onto the gravel road; the red and orange marks, and NST rectangles, turn left into forest, following the shoreline of a second pond. Unless you're planning only a 2-mile walk, stay with the red and orange blazes.

This pond is Wilbur Pond, a busy place in summer but tranquil and picturesque in other seasons. The trail, running through more hemlock groves, follows the shore for about $\frac{1}{2}$ mile, going up and down several small hills and often running at the water's edge. Some camps can be seen across the pond but your chances of finding ducks, geese, or other waterfowl here are excellent, especially in autumn.

At the end of a small cove, the trail turns away from the pond and goes uphill, to the right, into a hardwood segment with more undergrowth than found in the hemlocks. In this section, the red trail and NST break off to the right; take that path if you're looking for a 6-mile walk. This connector segment crosses a gravel road and runs past numerous stone walls and rock piles that show the area was once farmland. It then rejoins the orange trail and the two run together again for the last 2-plus miles of the walk. However, the red trail misses the best hemlock groves,

Parts of Walkabout Trail are rocky and hilly.

the ski trail, and the wildlife marsh, although the NST passes the marsh as it continues north.

Those continuing on the orange trail head left and leave the rocky areas for a while, walking on an easy, flat path. You enter an area where a forest management study has been conducted for several years. Many trees have metal plates nailed to them. You'll start crossing gravel roads (popular in winter as cross-country ski trails) and also pass into Pulaski Park, although no signs show the dividing line.

One of the open roads, about 3½ miles from your start, is marked with triangular red blazes, indicating it is a ski trail that originates at Peck Pond in Pulaski Park (see Walk 27). For a short distance, you will walk this road, going down a hill and then over a wide bridge. Just beyond the bridge, an orange arrow on a tree and a sign indicate the Walkabout turns to the right while the ski trail goes ahead. The sign says the distance back to the GW (George Washington) Campground is 5 miles. Take heart; it's only about 4½ miles.

Again walking on a path blazed only in orange, you are in an easy segment. The trail runs parallel to a gravel road for almost ½ mile before crossing the road (it is marked with yellow and blue-green ski blazes) and heading downhill into another grove of towering, impressive hemlocks. Soon, the trail narrows considerably and eventually you return to rocky and slightly hilly terrain. When you emerge from this section onto another gravel road, you are near one of the highlights of this walk.

As soon as you cross this road you'll see the marsh off to your left. The trail runs along the shore for a short distance, then turns left at the open, grassy dike that created the marsh. You have now gone 5 miles, and this is a great place to take a rest break. The marsh attracts much wildlife, including swallows, kingfishers, wood ducks (which are lured by wooden nesting boxes installed on poles above the water), muskrats, minks, and raccoons. In some years, beavers also live in the marsh. A lodge can be seen near the left shore, as you face the marsh from the dike, and other evidence of their presence can be found in cone-shaped stumps and chewed-off twigs.

When you're ready to resume the walk, cross the dike to the far end and return to the woods. Almost immediately, the trail splits. Stay left. In just over ½ mile, your path will be joined by the red trail coming in from the right. The walking is easy at first, then becomes more up-and-down and crosses several damp areas where you may have to pick your way, even in summer and fall, by stepping on rocks and exposed roots.

From the time the red trail rejoins your path, it is more than ½ mile until you cross the next gravel road. Go straight across the road and you are entering the final segment. Here, you will see the largest boulders along the Walkabout, many of them covered with lichens or mosses. The trail gradually runs downhill into a lovely but damp area of big hemlocks and laurel. One section of this wet area is equipped with hundreds of short logs lying crosswise, creating a miniature version of an old-fashioned corduroy road and serving as a walkway. When you reach the end of this walkway, you are at the foot of a rather steep hill.

Go up the hill and you'll see the blue trail coming in from the right. Now, once again following triple blazes, you have an easy ½-mile walk on a worn, mostly downhill path back to your car at the beach.

27 · Pulaski Park–Peck Pond

Walking distance: 3 miles
Walking time: 1½ to 2 hours

This is an easy 3-mile walk that begins and ends at a beach and picnic area. Highlights include an old-fashioned covered bridge, views of a pond, many kinds of trees, and a couple of water holes built decades ago for fighting forest fires.

The route described here is actually a state-managed cross-country ski trail, one of the most popular in the area, so walkers would not be welcome in snow season. However, the trail is a pleasure in all other seasons. It's dry enough for spring walking, it's open and airy for summer strolls, and it has the right mixture of trees for fall foliage visits. Remember, however, that this is a state property and most of it is open to hunting in fall. State law requires visitors to wear orange from October through February.

There are four ski trails, marked in pink (½ mile), red (2 miles), blue-green (3 miles), and yellow (4 miles). You can walk any of them, but I recommend the 3-miler. The pink trail is too short and runs through the picnic area, likely to be busy in summer and fall. The red trail is pretty but misses the covered bridge. The yellow trail is the same as the blue-green trail except for an extra loop that seems to add little other than distance.

For a short, pleasant walk, you also can simply walk around Peck Pond, the park's centerpiece. A path blazed in white circles the pond. This walk would be about 1½ miles.

Although the area is commonly known as Pulaski Park, the proper name is the Casimir Pulaski Memorial Recreation Area. It is in western Glocester, nudging the Connecticut border. In addition to hiking and skiing, the park offers swimming, fishing, picnicking, and various other sport activities. User fees are charged in summer and during ski season.

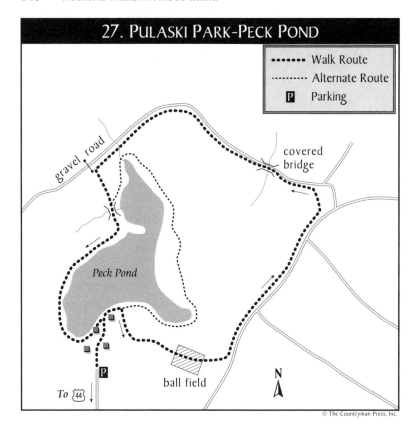

27. PULASKI PARK-PECK POND

●●●●●● Walk Route
·········· Alternate Route
P Parking

gravel road

covered bridge

Peck Pond

P

ball field

N

To (44)

© The Countryman Press, Inc.

Access

To reach the park entrance, take US 44 west from Chepachet, go past Bowdish Reservoir, the State Line Restaurant, and a camping area, and turn right onto Pulaski Road. Look for the park sign and an entrance road veering off to the right. Continue driving to the end of the entrance road, where there are large parking areas and some buildings.

Trail

From the parking lot, walk down to the pond and head to the right side of the beach. Just beyond a pavilion that doubles as a warm-up hut in winter, look for the triangular blazes that mark the start of the ski trails. The white-blazed pond walk also begins here.

All four ski trails run together at first, going uphill from the pond through a grove of tall pines. The red trail shoots off first; at that junction, turn right. Quickly, the pink trail also cuts off, just before you emerge from the pines into a park softball field.

Follow the left edge of the clearing to pick up the blue-green blazes again on the far side of the field. From there, it's just a few steps to a gravel lane. Turn left. You'll be on this lane and similar ones for most of the walk.

This section is an old forest of mostly pines and oaks. You will soon pass a sign that indicates you are entering the George Washington Management Area and then another sign that notes a forest study was done here on gypsy moths and their long-term effects on trees. In the 1970s and 1980s there were heavy moth infestations here and many trees were defoliated. The study ran from 1987 to 1997. Few indications remain of the study and most of the trees you pass look healthy indeed.

About the time you see an arrow that shows the yellow trail is breaking off, you will pass an orange-blazed path that crosses your road. This is part of the Walkabout Trail (Walk 26) and later you will cross it again. The yellow ski trail goes off to the right on a woods lane and rejoins your route in about ¼ mile on still another lane. After the yellow trail rejoins the blue-green route, the two trails run together the rest of the way.

When you reach a Y-junction, look for the triangular blazes going to the left. You will leave the open lane for a wide ski/hiking path that runs downhill. This is a favorite segment for skiers. After the short descent, you reach another gravel lane. Turning left here is easy for walkers, but the 90-degree turn at the bottom of the hill is a challenge for cross-country skiers.

Just ahead is the covered bridge, built in the early 1980s in the style of 18th- and 19th-century bridges. It spans a picturesque little brook and is an ideal place to rest for a while, since you are roughly midway in your walk.

There are numerous hemlocks in this area as well as enough hardwoods, bushes, and ferns to make for colorful walking in fall.

Peck Pond is a good place for a relaxing visit.

Beyond the bridge, the lane curves often, running primarily downhill. At the bottom of a slope, look on the left for a small circular water hole built long ago in case of forest fires. Later you'll pass a larger one lined with stones.

Midway through a horseshoe bend, you should notice the orange-blazed Walkabout Trail footpath again crossing the gravel lane. It runs parallel to your lane, on the left, for a short distance. The next landmark is the return of the red-blazed trail (it joins from the left), and, soon after, at the bottom of another slope, you'll find the larger stone-lined water hole, also on the left.

On the uphill climb, watch for the triangular ski blazes pointing to a path off to the left. It is just before a metal gate. Take this path through a pretty area that includes stone walls and a bridge and emerges on a trail that runs along Peck Pond. You are across from the beach area, and benches here make it another place to linger. The trail follows the shoreline to the right, crosses a bridge at the pond's dam, and takes you back to where you began.

28 · Buck Hill

Walking distance: 6 miles
Walking time: 3 to 3½ hours

Buck Hill is a good place to visit if you want to combine walking with wildlife watching, a bit of historical perspective, and a sense of accomplishment. After all, how often can you hike into three states in a couple of hours? In fact, on this walk, you'll find the granite post that marks the precise spot where Rhode Island, Connecticut, and Massachusetts meet.

The 1,800-acre Buck Hill Wildlife Management Area is in Burrillville, the extreme northwestern corner of the state. And there has been plenty of "management" of this forest, including the construction of a large marsh and several tiny ponds and the cultivation of numerous small grain patches. The result has been an abundance of wildlife, including deer, foxes, raccoons, coyotes, rabbits, squirrels, ruffed grouse, wild turkeys, ducks, geese, herons, owls, hawks, and dozens of species of songbirds. What you see may depend on when you go and how observant—and lucky—you are.

The 6-mile route described here visits the marsh and some of the ponds and fields. It also cuts through a rocky forest, then follows ancient woods roads. You'll loop up to the Massachusetts state line, visit the tri-state boundary post, then follow the Connecticut state line briefly before returning to Buck Hill's management roads. Shortcuts are possible, although they would eliminate the boundary post.

Buck Hill is probably most attractive in spring and fall, but remember that this area draws numerous hunters in October, November, and December.

28. BUCK HILL

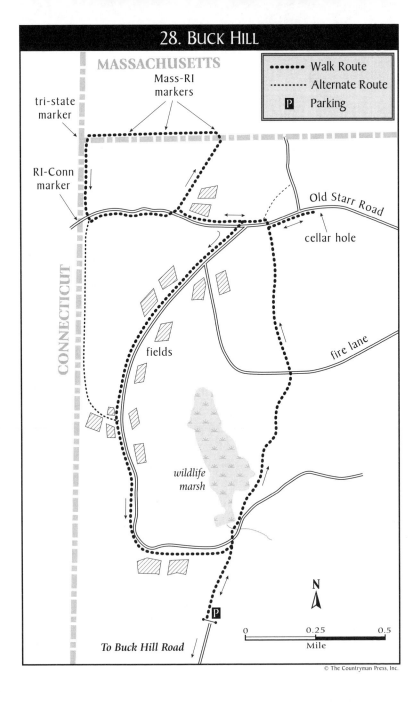

MASSACHUSETTS

Mass-RI markers

tri-state marker

RI-Conn marker

CONNECTICUT

Old Starr Road

cellar hole

fire lane

fields

wildlife marsh

•••••• Walk Route
•••••• Alternate Route
P Parking

N

0   0.25   0.5
Mile

P

To Buck Hill Road

© The Countryman Press, Inc.

Access

To reach the entrance road, take RI 100 north from Pascoag to Buck Hill Road and turn left. Watch your odometer; the entrance, beside a small sign, is 2.3 miles from the turnoff. You will pass a fire tower and a road to a Boy Scout camp on your left, then a rifle range on the right. The gravel access road is also on the right.

During most of the year you can drive only 0.3 mile from the paved road before being stopped at a gate. The management roads are open for driving during hunting season, but that is not a good time for hikers to be roaming the woods, so I suggest you wait until late winter or go in spring, summer, or early fall, even if you have to walk a little farther.

Trail

From the parking area, pass the gate and follow the entrance road. One of the tiny ponds is immediately on your left, and the gravel road is flanked with young pines. In about ⅓ mile you'll reach a road coming in from the left; it will be your return route. Continuing straight ahead, you cross a small brook and soon see a short lane to the left going to an earthen dam and the marsh. Take a few minutes and look over this marsh, built to accommodate wildlife. Numerous wood duck boxes have been erected over the water, and you are likely to see many birds here, ranging from swallows to ducks to herons. At times beavers have lived in the marsh, and other mammals visit it regularly. Hundreds of trees were drowned by the water and their standing skeletons can give the place a slightly eerie appearance, particularly if you visit in twilight shadows or at dawn, when mists swirl around the old trees.

Continue following the lane around the right (east) side of the marsh. Ignore a road that goes to the right; it eventually runs off state property. After reaching another open spot that gives good views of the water, the lane dwindles to a narrow footpath which at this writing is blazed in weak yellow and enters a rocky forest. This path, strewn with rocks and slightly uphill, is one of the few segments of the hike not on open roads. It weaves for about ½ mile before emerging on a fire lane. You could turn left on

Three states merge at this marker at Buck Hill.

this lane for a shortcut (see map) but I recommend simply crossing the lane and staying on the narrow path. In this next area you start seeing stone walls, reminders that this was once farmland, and in less than ½ mile from the fire lane you break out onto another road.

This is Old Starr Road, one of the earliest roadways in this area. Bounded on both sides by stone walls, it is worn deep into the forest floor. The yellow-marked footpath goes directly across this road but I suggest turning right on the road, going just 50 yards or so (passing another road on your left) and looking just off Old Starr Road on your right for a small cellar hole. This, legends say, was the home of the area's first white resident.

Now you're ready to search for the tri-state marker. Retrace your steps back on Old Starr Road (heading west), past the spot where the yellow trail left the forest. The road dips through a low area, then reaches a wide, grassy lane curving left. Pass it (later you will return to it) and also ignore an opening a short distance ahead that goes into a field on the right. Instead, continue walking straight west even though the path becomes narrow and overgrown. In about 200 yards, the path opens considerably and you'll see a trail angling off to the right. Here you have a choice, because both the trail ahead and the path to the right can lead to the marker. For this walk, turn to the right; you'll return on the main trail.

This side trail angles back northeast for a short distance, going over some low ridges, then dropping slightly downhill. When you reach a side trail on the left, look to the right for the first state marker, a stone post that says RI on one side and MASS on the other. Signs on a tree also indicate this is the state line. Turn left now, and take this hilly, rocky path left and you will pass two more similar posts. Finally, this path reaches a small knoll where there is a small clearing. In the center is a 4-foot-high granite marker with RI, MASS, and CONN chiseled into its sides and the year 1883. This is a good place to rest; you've walked approximately 3 miles.

Several trails run downhill from the marker; take the one, blazed in faded white, that goes to the left of the path you were walking. It drops through a low area and, about ⅓ mile later, reaches another state boundary marker. This one is an upright field stone with RI on one side and CONN on the other, standing beside an old road. This road is the Old Starr Road you were walking earlier. Turn left from the marker.

(An alternative, if you prefer woods walking, is to go directly across Old Starr Road at the RI–CONN marker, following the state line. This is an easy trail and a slightly shorter route back to the main management road. It is a pleasant enough walk but unremarkable. After ⅔ mile, you reach a trail crossroads beside a yellow sign that says NO UNAUTHORIZED VEHICLES BEYOND THIS POINT, one of several such signs in the area. Turn left at the crossing and you'll soon reach a small grain field, then another, and the road.)

If, like me, you would rather have opportunities for seeing more wildlife, walk Old Starr Road and in about ⅓ mile you will be back at the junction that took you to the Massachusetts line. Rewalk the narrow, overgrown path and then turn right onto the grassy lane that is Buck Hill's main access road. You'll pass small ponds, with wood duck houses, and numerous small clearings that are fields cut from the forest. Many are planted in grain for wildlife and this area is your best chance for seeing deer, coyotes, pheasants, turkeys, and other wild creatures. Each field is screened from the lane by trees, but each has an entrance lane that enables you to take a look. However, return to the main road each time to resume walking.

This 1½-mile road eventually curves to the left and goes from grassy to woodsy. The road takes you back to the gravel entrance road. Your car is to the right, but you might want to visit the marsh (now on your left) once more before leaving. It's a great place to rest and watch Buck Hill's wildlife.

29 · Black Hut

Walking distance: 2¾ miles
Walking time: 2 hours

If you are looking for a quiet woods walk, with time and space to linger and look, give Black Hut a try. There you can roam for miles with little chance of running into other hikers, and maybe not any other people at all, unless it is hunting season.

The Black Hut Wildlife Management Area in Burrillville is big, more than 1,500 acres, but has been overlooked by most Rhode Island outdoors enthusiasts. It does draw its share of hunters in late fall and early winter, and some trail bikers and horseback riders, but quite often hikers will have the huge forest all to themselves.

The only problem for hikers is that there are no marked trails at Black Hut, and while the old roads are easy to walk, it is difficult to make a loop walk because most of the roads simply run off state property. Still, the 2¾-mile walk described here is very pleasant. It visits a wildlife marsh, runs along small fields planted for the wild creatures, goes as far as a hurrying little stream, then circles through quiet forest. At all three turnaround points, the ambitious can explore farther if they wish, so the walk could be considerably longer than outlined here.

Spring is probably the best season for visiting Black Hut because of bird activity, wildflowers, and the chance of seeing other wild creatures.

Access

Black Hut lies almost on the Massachusetts line in Burrillville. Take RI 102 north from Chepachet or south from Slatersville and turn off at the village of Glendale. Use an unmarked road beside the Bella Restaurant. If coming

29. BLACK HUT

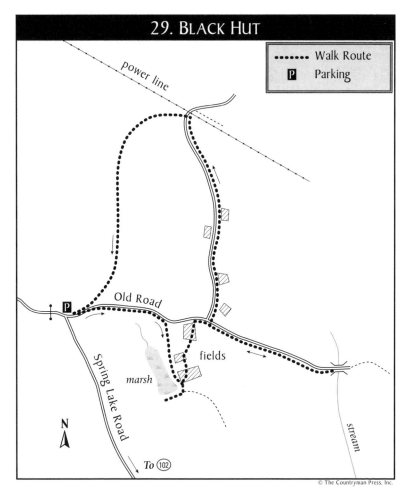

Walk Route
P Parking

Power line

Old Road

P

fields

marsh

Spring Lake Road

N

To 102

stream

© The Countryman Press, Inc.

from Chepachet, the turnoff is 3.8 miles from the traffic light at US 44 or 1 mile beyond a light at RI 107. After leaving RI 102, take the first right, cross a river, and again take the first right, Joslin Road, and pass under RI 102. Follow Joslin Road 0.2 mile north to the first road on the left, Spring Lake Road. Follow Spring Lake Road 1.8 miles (it eventually changes from pavement to dirt) to its end at a parking area in the forest.

Trail

Old lanes run both left and right from the parking area. The barricaded lane to the left once was a continuation of Spring Lake Road; now it is merely a narrow path. Take the wider lane running to the right (ignore the many motorcycle paths in this area).

Around the first bend you reach an orange barway. Just beyond this gate is a path entering from the left; this will be your return route. For now, stay on the wide lane, which actually was a roadway many decades ago. This lane is somewhat curvy at its start. It used to be flanked by tall trees but recent logging removed many of the larger trees on the left side. However, big trees—mostly oaks and maples with a healthy sprinkling of sassafras, pines, and birches—remain along the right side.

About $\frac{1}{4}$ mile from your start, the road forks; go to the right. You soon are walking parallel to the 3-acre wildlife marsh, on your right, but the views here are obscured by surging young pines. On the left you begin passing the first of the little grain plots planted for wildlife. Go slowly and quietly; deer, foxes, coyotes, rabbits, birds, and butterflies use these fields. At $\frac{1}{2}$ mile from your start, you reach the dike that helped create the marsh. Here, just to the right of the lane, are your best views of the marsh, which often attracts waterfowl and other birds as well as mammals, frogs, and other forms of wildlife.

There is a temptation here to continue following the lane, which at the dike turns to the left, into the woods. You can follow it if you wish, but it eventually runs back out to Spring Lake Road, and you would have to retrace your steps or follow the pavement back. Instead, go into the little field nearest the dike, look for an opening in a stone wall along the left (west) side of the field, and follow the narrow path you find there. It runs into woods but quickly leads to a second, very small field. Go along the right edge of this field and you will soon walk into a third field, which will lead you back to the entrance road (Old Road). Or, if finding your way through these little fields sounds too complicated, simply rewalk the lane beside the marsh back to the junction you reached earlier.

Small marsh attracts wildlife at Black Hut.

The main roadway beyond the fields was perhaps the most pleasant part of Black Hut when it was shaded by tall, majestic trees. However, even with many of these trees gone, it remains interesting with stone walls and the birdlife attracted by the burgeoning new growth of bushes and saplings. Walking this road also requires some backtracking but it is usually worthwhile.

Shortly after reaching this road from the fields and turning right, you will see another wide lane going off to the left; you'll walk it later. Stay on the main road for another ⅓ mile beyond the side lane and you will reach the stream, crossed by a plank bridge. In spring, this stream usually runs high and fast and is extremely picturesque. The road continues beyond the bridge but eventually runs off state property, so a turnaround here is recommended.

Return to the intersection with the other lane, now on your right. There are a couple of garden-sized clearings along the first segment of this lane and several more later. Like the main road, the lane is open and easy to walk, although there may be a few wet places. It is another good segment for birds with such forest species as chickadees, nuthatches, kinglets, and thrushes often seen.

Just as you reach a power-line strip, you will pass a trail joining the lane from the left. This will be your return toward the parking lot, but before turning, go a few steps farther and look over the clearing. Power-line strips are the closest things to wild meadows in many areas now, and you may see bluebirds, hawks, and butterflies here as well as numerous varieties of wildflowers. At this point you have gone only about 1¾ miles, but the ambitious can wander up and down the power line to their heart's content before turning back.

When ready for the final leg, return to the trail junction just before the power line. This is more of a path than a lane but no less pleasant. This path of about 1 mile begins in pines and runs through varying stands of trees and bushes, including some mountain laurel. It has some minor ups and downs and you will see several stone walls, some straight and solid, others erratic and tumbling. At one point the trail skirts the right end of a stone wall; when you pass this wall you are nearing the main road. And when you reach this road, it is just a few steps to the right back to your car.

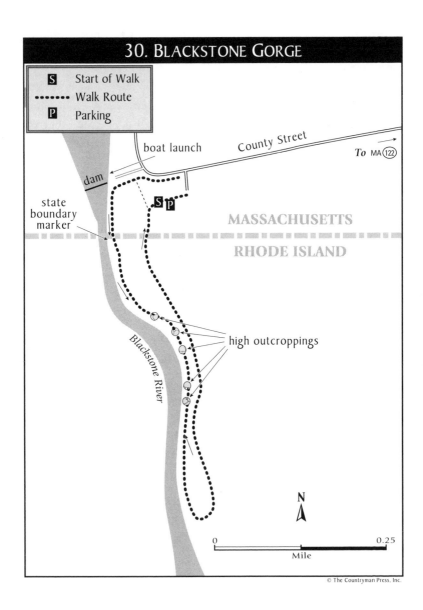

30. BLACKSTONE GORGE

S Start of Walk
•••••• Walk Route
P Parking

boat launch
County Street
To MA 122

dam

state
boundary
marker

S P

MASSACHUSETTS

RHODE ISLAND

high outcroppings

Blackstone River

N

0   0.25
Mile

© The Countryman Press, Inc.

30 · Blackstone Gorge

Walking distance: 1¼ miles
Walking time: 1 to 2 hours

This place is for walkers who enjoy scenery, rock hopping, and maybe a dash of daring. It is not a place for hikers looking for a lot of miles. The trails here are short but they are spectacular.

For years, it was called High Rocks Gorge for the huge, imposing out-croppings that loom above the twisting, churning Blackstone River. Now the rocky chute is the featured attraction of Blackstone Gorge Bi-State Park, part of the Blackstone River Valley National Heritage Corridor. As the name implies, the park spills across the Massachusetts–Rhode Island border. Some 160 acres of the park lie in Rhode Island and 86 are in Massachusetts. Although access is from Massachusetts, nearly all of the gorge itself is in Rhode Island.

Unfortunately, at this writing, none of the trails are marked and there is no footbridge that would enable visitors to cross to the largest segment of the park. However, a series of paths made by generations of admirers run to all the high bluffs along one side of the gorge and also down to many dramatic vistas along the river.

People who have seen the Blackstone River only where it flows through cities and towns, or know how it was harnessed for industry through numerous dams, might have trouble believing a gorge like this still exists. It has been called "the last untamed stretch of the river," and when the water is running high, "untamed" might be an understatement. It roars and tumbles over thousands of rocks and ledges as it crashes through the deep, narrow gorge.

I find the gorge most appealing in winter and early spring, when snowmelt often sends additional water into the rapids and icy fringes cling to the rocks, but climbing the outcroppings can be dangerous in those times. Be safe. If the rocks are slippery, come back another day for your bolder exploring.

Access

Blackstone Gorge Bi-State Park is at the end of County Street in the Massachusetts village of Blackstone. Drive RI 122 north through Woonsocket or reach Route 122 in Massachusetts from RI 146A in North Smithfield by way of St. Paul Street. Signs for the Gorge along MA 122 in Blackstone will lead you to County Street and then to a parking lot near the river.

Trail

From the parking lot, go directly down to the river for a good look at Rolling Dam, which controls the water pouring into the gorge. Just to the right of the dam is a canoe launch and calm water. To the left are the first of the rapids.

Two trails run along the river, occasionally merging, and it is tempting to call them the higher trail and the lower trail, because they begin that way. But the lower trail, which initially allows visitors to go right to the shoreline, eventually climbs the highest bluffs above the gorge. Let's just say that the path closest to the water provides the best views, the most strenuous scrambling, and, when the rocks are wet or icy, the most danger. The trail running a short distance from the bluffs is straighter and much safer, but remaining on it for your entire walk would prevent you from experiencing what makes the gorge so spectacular and fascinating. This walk combines them in a loop, beginning on the "lower" trail.

Shortly after your start, within yards of the dam, you cross the state line into Rhode Island. If you are near the water you can find the concrete post with MASS on one side and RI on the other.

The paths run past hemlocks and mountain laurel bushes as they begin ascending toward the bluffs. Frequent cutoffs to the right go down

Water roars through the Blackstone Gorge.

to the water and, when the water level is down, the nimble sometimes can cross the river on exposed rocks. However, don't try this when the water is high or rocks are icy.

As a general rule, the farther you go, the higher the bluffs are above the river. In some cases, getting onto the outcroppings is an easy matter. In others, it takes more effort and determination. Always stay away from the edges. A fall would be long and disastrous.

Not all of the outcroppings provide good views, because of surrounding trees and bushes, but many do. In places, you can see the rapids frothing below and to the right and the much calmer river flowing away far to the left. Across the river are more ledges, although not as high or rugged as those you are standing on, and dense forest.

Numerous paths circle down around the ledges to the river, and going to the base of the outcroppings can add new perspectives, but these paths are not for everybody. They are steep and can be extremely slippery. Also, keep in mind that getting back up might be more difficult than getting down.

Still, if you are agile, go down to the water below the outcroppings. Sit on a rock, listen to the roar, and watch the water cascade by. Occasionally you might see a fish rise. I once watched a mink hunting along the shore. Mostly, though, it is a great place to simply admire the topography of the place, high granite walls towering above you on both sides of hurrying rapids.

Back on the bluffs, just when it seems the trail along the top is flattening, you will reach the most imposing ledge, a bulging rock some 70 or 80 feet above the water. From here, looking down and to the left, you'll see the river suddenly become smooth as it leaves the rocky bed. Shortly beyond this point, the river leaves the park itself.

You can return by taking the worn and more direct parallel trail or spend some time exploring other paths that weave through the woods a short distance back from the bluffs. However, many of these woods paths are confusing, and they certainly lack the drama of the riverside trails. I recommend revisiting the high rocks on your way back. It's hard to get too much of those places.

31 · Fort Nature Refuge

Walking distance: 3¾ miles
Walking time: 2½ hours

A quiet, beckoning oasis in North Smithfield is gradually being discovered by Rhode Island walkers. Officially the Florence Sutherland Fort & Richard Knight Fort Nature Refuge at Primrose Ledges, this onetime farm is now a surging forest turned over to wildlife.

Part of the refuge system of the Audubon Society of Rhode Island, the Fort Nature Refuge consists of approximately 235 acres and includes three ponds, all made by the Fort family, which had created its own wildlife sanctuary before donating the property to Audubon in 1997. The 3¾-mile walk described here visits all three ponds, mostly on open, easy-to-walk lanes. The route includes two loops joined by a yellow-marked connector that crosses a power line. Shorter walks are available as well.

This is a nature preserve in the basic sense of the term and the many facets of nature are the chief attractions. As you wander the lanes you are likely to see many birds, possibly including wild turkeys, grouse, owls, and various songbirds. Fort is also known for its mammals; I've seen deer, coyotes, otters, beavers, minks, muskrats, rabbits, red squirrels, gray squirrels, flying squirrels, chipmunks, white-footed mice, and bats here, plus tracks of fishers and foxes. In warmer seasons you are likely to find ducks and herons at the ponds, along with dragonflies, butterflies, frogs, turtles, and numerous wildflowers, including immense stands of water lilies.

The mammals and their tracks, and the abundance of pines and hemlocks, make the refuge an interesting and attractive place to visit in snow. The relatively flat lanes make it excellent for cross-country skiing as well

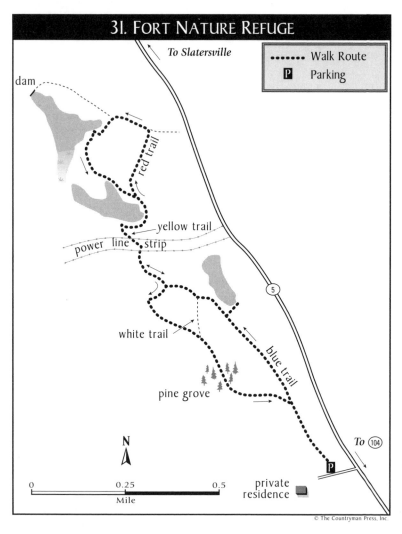

31. FORT NATURE REFUGE

To Slatersville

•••••• Walk Route

P Parking

dam

red trail

yellow trail

power line strip

white trail

5

blue trail

pine grove

To 104

P

private residence

N

0   0.25   0.5
Mile

© The Countryman Press, Inc.

as walking. It is also a prime winter and fall destination because, as an Audubon Society property, no hunting is allowed. As with all Audubon refuges, visitors are asked to remain on the trails and to leave dogs at home.

Access

The Fort Nature Refuge is on RI 5 in North Smithfield. The entrance lane is 0.4 mile north of RI 5's intersection with RI 104, just beyond the Primrose fire station, or 3 miles south of the village of Slatersville. As you proceed up the lane, look for a grassy parking area and kiosk on the west. The entrance lane is gated beyond the parking lot because it leads to a private residence.

Trail

The trail begins just to the right of the kiosk among small pines. In moments, you are on an old lane, one of the many tractor lanes used by the Fort family when it farmed the land and later made it into a wildlife sanctuary. As soon as you begin walking the lane you'll see a blue-blazed path coming down a slope on the left; this will be your return route. For now, walk the flat, nearly straight lane that runs through dense forest. For much of this early part, the lane is flanked by tall trees. Where the trees are considerably smaller you are passing former fields now returning to forest. Here, as throughout your walk, you are likely to see deer or coyote tracks on the path.

In about ½ mile you reach a cutoff path to the right. Take this for your first look at a pond. The short path ends at the shore. Approach quietly; this pond often harbors wood ducks and other waterbirds and perhaps otters. In summer it is ringed with water lilies.

Back on the blue trail, you begin going slightly uphill as the trail curves left and then reaches a fork. A path blazed in white goes to the left; take it only if you want a very short walk. For this walk, remain on the blue trail. The lane is flanked in places by rocky ridges and you will cross a small brook on a low stone bridge. After passing an unmarked lane on the right, begin looking, also on the right, for the yellow-blazed connector path. Skipping the connector and the red-blazed second loop will give you a walk of less than 2 miles but you would miss two of the refuge's three ponds.

The yellow connector quickly takes you out of the forest into a strip cleared for a power line. Pause here and look around; these clearings often

Beavers leave their signs at the Fort Refuge.

contain birds and wildflowers you cannot find in the forest. The trail crosses the strip and a motorcycle trail, then returns to forest on another old lane. Soon, though, it breaks off to the right into a dense hemlock thicket, then emerges in moments into a field returning to forest. This is a good opportunity to see which bushes and trees take over when a field is abandoned.

After running along the right edge of this old field briefly, the trail turns to the right and cuts through another hemlock grove, angling downhill toward the second pond. After passing a group of glacial rocks called erratics, you drop down to the pond's shore. This pond has even more water lilies than the first, plus numerous frogs, turtles, and wood duck nesting boxes. Until 2005, a family of beavers lived in this pond and evidence of their work remains in numerous chewed trees and stumps.

The trail skirts the edge of the pond, then goes onto a grassy dike. A bench on the dike provides a good viewing spot. Shortly beyond this opening, the yellow trail terminates at the beginning of the red loop. It can be a short loop, about ½ mile, or extended another ½ mile by going to the dam for the third pond and back. Obviously you can go around the loop either way but for this walk go right at the trail junction.

There are side trails along this loop; ignore them and remain with the red blazes. You will soon reach a well-worn lane and curve to the left. When the lane splits, you have a choice. The right fork will take you to the dam at the far end of the third pond and its best viewing spot. Otters, beavers, and ducks all use the third pond at times. However, you will have to return on the same path to this junction. When back at the junction, continue to the right on the red trail. A short distance up this path look for a faint, unmarked cutoff on your right. Beginning in a stand of young birches, this detour takes you to the third pond's shallow end, a place decorated in spring and summer with blooming water plants and often sheltering herons and other birds.

The red trail itself wanders through more young forest, a great place for songbirds, and then skirts the edge of the second pond (no good views) on its return toward the yellow connector trail. After backtracking on the yellow trail past the bench end of the second pond and across the power line strip, you return to the blue loop. Now turn right.

This is an easy, pleasant section with surging ferns on the ground beneath tall pines. The trail swings left and gradually climbs a low ridge. Here, on the left, you see the largest boulders on this walk. The lane continues running through the pine grove until reaching the junction with the white trail, coming in from the left. For the next ¼ mile or so you are walking with a grove of pines on your left and mixed woods on the right. When the trail turns left and angles over a ridge, you are nearing the end of your walk. This path emerges on the grassy lane you walked earlier. The parking lot and your car are just to the right.

32. Lime Rock Preserve

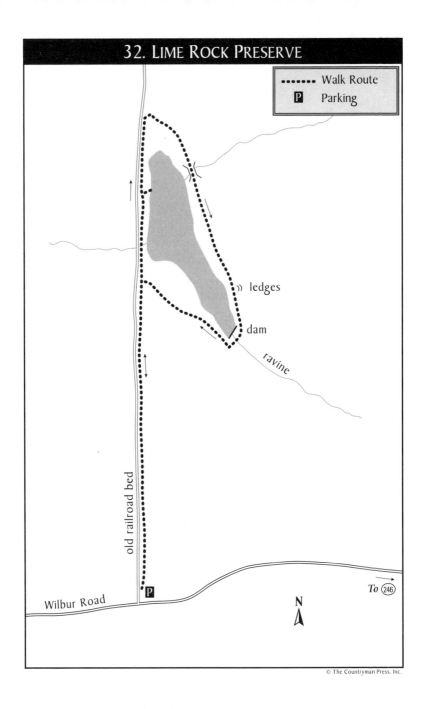

Walk Route
P Parking

ledges

dam

ravine

old railroad bed

Wilbur Road

P

To (246)

N

© The Countryman Press, Inc.

32 · Lime Rock Preserve

Walking distance: 2 miles
Walking time: 1 to 1½ hours

This is a jewel among Rhode Island public places. Walkers who appreciate botany and geology will love it because Lime Rock has more unusual plants and types of stone than any other place in the state. There are usually plenty of birds here, too.

In this preserve in Lincoln, the sharp-eyed may find numerous wildflowers, particularly in spring. Some 30 rare plant species thrive on this preserve, including many found nowhere else in the state. Even the more casual walkers are likely to see such flowers as marsh marigolds, bluets, wood anemones, bellworts, and nodding trilliums. An unusually high level of limestone in the soil is credited with sustaining the lush plant life, which also includes wide varieties of trees, bushes, and vines. A visit in May is recommended for seeing the best variety of blooming plants.

People who like rocks and stones will have their own challenge in trying to identify the various ledges and boulders. Among other stones, Lime Rock includes, as a sign at the entrance says, RHODE ISLAND'S MOST EXTENSIVE OUTCROPPING OF MARBLE.

However, you don't have to be a flower or rock enthusiast to enjoy the preserve. It is simply an interesting place to walk. The route outlined here, just under 2 miles in length, begins and ends on an old railroad bed, swings around a picturesque pond, passes imposing ledges, crosses brooks, and wanders through a fern-carpeted, rock-strewn forest.

In order to preserve the plants, The Nature Conservancy, which owns most of the property, asks that visitors stay on the paths and, of course, avoid picking or disturbing any plants.

Wildflower enthusiasts are drawn to Lime Rock.

Access

From RI 116 (accessible from I-295 or RI 146) look for RI 246 virtually across from the Lincoln Mall shopping center. The road runs parallel to and virtually in the shadow of the much busier RI 146. Take RI 246 south about a mile to Wilbur Road and turn right. The Lime Rock Preserve and a small parking area are about 0.5 mile on your right.

Trail

You begin on a straight path that a century ago was an electric railroad running from Providence to Woonsocket. At the start the railroad bed is lower than the surrounding terrain; later it is high above both sides. This first segment often is wet; if there is too much water, simply climb the left shoulder and walk a narrow trail that parallels the old railroad bed.

Tall trees shade the lane, and off in the woods you can see rock outcroppings. Ferns dominate the undergrowth, but numerous other plants compete for growing room as well.

In less than ½ mile, you reach the pond, on your right. Best views of the water will come later, from the far side. Here the trail is high and offers good views, to the left, of a brook that flows far beneath you into the pond. Also, you can see some interesting conglomerate stone ledges and boulders on the left. In several places the railroad was cut through ledges, and now ferns and other plants grow out of the rock crevices.

A string of condominiums, perched high on a ridge to the left, may be visible through the trees as you pass the pond. Beyond the pond, start looking for the cutoff trail to the right. It is just beyond one of the sliced ledges. There are no blazes or markers but the side trail is well worn and easy to see. This side trail, which loops around the pond, might be the most attractive segment of the entire walk. You'll pass white boulders and dozens of kinds of trees and shrubs and cross a stone bridge. Just upstream from the bridge, if you are visiting in May, you should see many of the brilliant yellow marsh marigolds that grow at the edge of the brook.

Beyond the brook you walk downhill, through a delightful area, until, just after passing a high ledge on your left, the path curves to the right and crosses the pond's earthen dam. (Ignore the several paths going to the left; they run off the preserve.) The dam provides a great look at the pond on your right. Below, on the left, is the tumbling brook that carries off the overflow.

At the end of the dam, follow the path that curves to the right, following the shoreline. This is another great section. The trail soon swings away from the water running beneath tall trees and curves around boulders. It eventually runs parallel to a stone wall and then rejoins the old railroad bed you walked earlier. Your car is to the left.

33 · Powder Mill Ledges Wildlife Refuge

Walking distance: 2 miles
Walking time: 1½ to 2 hours

Powder Mill Ledges is the name given to the Audubon Society wildlife refuge in Smithfield, and it is rapidly gaining popularity as a walking place. The woodsy hill property, crisscrossed with old stone walls, has three trail loops that total just under 2 miles.

The site is also the headquarters of the Audubon Society of Rhode Island, and visitors are asked to register at the building before walking the trails. Spending some time inside the center is recommended anyway because of the wealth of information available on area wildlife and the state's environment. Also, you can pick up a brochure that describes the property and includes a trail map.

Don't look for a powder mill (the one for which the property was named is believed to have been a considerable distance farther west) or massive ledges. There are some rock outcroppings but none on the scale of those found in other areas of the state. Still, this is an excellent place for a leisurely, nature-oriented walk. The route described here includes all three loops and goes though several types of forest as well as visiting grassy meadows and a tiny pond and crossing an open power-line strip that attracts numerous birds. Also, as might be expected at an Audubon Society headquarters, the many birdhouses erected throughout the property make seeing birds even more likely.

Although this is something of an urban refuge, chances of seeing wildlife, in addition to songbirds, are usually good. Chipmunks and squirrels abound in the woods, and deer, foxes, wild turkeys, and owls are known to live on the property.

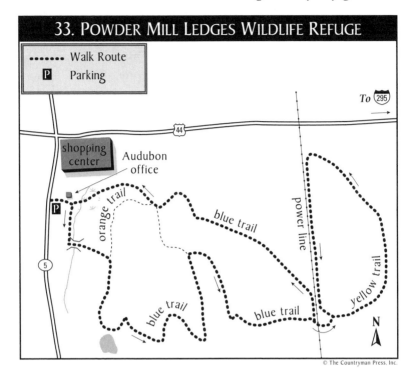

33. POWDER MILL LEDGES WILDLIFE REFUGE

•••••• Walk Route

P Parking

© The Countryman Press, Inc.

The trail provides easy walking although there is a relatively steep slope early in the walk, and some sections include rocky surfaces. As with all Audubon Society properties, visitors are asked to remain on marked trails.

Access

Take US 44 into the village of Greenville, then turn south on RI 5 (Sanderson Road). The Audubon Society headquarters building and a large parking lot are a short distance on the left.

Trail

Just beyond the building is an information kiosk, and the trail begins behind the kiosk. It goes to the right, along a grassy area. Keep an eye on the fence that borders the little field; numerous birdhouses are nailed to posts, and in nesting season you are likely to see birds here, perhaps even the lovely bluebirds.

This path, blazed in orange, enters the woods over a small bridge and soon splits. For this walk, go to the right, following one of the many stone walls you will be seeing. They show that this land once was cleared and used as fields and pastures.

A boardwalk takes you past a small pond, and then you start climbing the hill, curling to the right, and then back left as you mount the ridge. For the most part, this is a section of tall pines with other species sprinkled about. Ferns are thick in summer.

When you reach a trail junction, about ⅓ mile into your walk, follow a blue arrow to the right. (The orange trail goes left, back downhill.) Now you are going through the refuge's interior, an attractive mixture of vibrant young pines, older hardwoods, and an abundance of bushes and shrubs. Here, you should see the woods birds—thrushes, woodpeckers, chickadees, and others.

At the power-line clearing, the blue trail turns left, but to walk the section on the far side of the wires, turn to the right. A narrow path crosses the clearing along a low wooden fence. Yellow blazes are painted on rocks. Hawks frequently hunt in the weedy strip, and you're likely to find towhees, thrashers, bluebirds, juncos, goldfinches, and other birds, depending on the season, along with wildflowers and bushes, including blueberries and blackberries.

As you re-enter woods on the far side, you'll find an abundance of new growth that has all but obliterated the remaining scars from a fire of several years ago. Larger boulders dot this section, and the trail is a bit rockier. In moments, you reach a second open strip, this one for a gas line, and the trail jogs to the left a few yards before returning to forest.

From here, the yellow trail makes a half-circle through a pleasant but unremarkable forest of oaks, hickories, beeches, and other hardwoods. The path re-emerges from the woods onto the gas line just a short distance above busy US 44. It then goes to the right a few steps and crosses a very thin strip of woods to the power-line clearing. You then take the

Children can handle most trails at Powder Mill Ledges.

power-line road to the left, uphill, to the narrow crossing trail you walked earlier. When you reach it, go right.

This takes you back to the blue trail. Pass the spot where you came out of the woods earlier, go another 40 yards or so along the edge of the forest, and follow the next blue arrow back into the woods on the left.

You are now returning to the pines, ferns, and stone walls and heading back downhill. There are a number of trees here with horizontal lines on them, scars from the days when they were used as posts for barbed wire fencing.

When the blue trail splits, go to the right (the left fork returns to the orange loop) and leave the woods through an opening in a high stone wall. Beyond the wall, the trails split once more. Going to the left would take you back to the bridge where you first entered the forest. Instead, take the right fork as it curls through a small meadow behind a shopping center and crosses a walkway over a marshy area on its way back to the Audubon headquarters.

34 • Rome Point

Walking distance: 2½ miles
Walking time: 2 hours

Rome Point, just south of Wickford in North Kingstown, is one of the few walking places in this book that might be more popular in winter than in the other seasons. The reason? Seals.

In winter, harbor seals migrate into Narragansett Bay from waters off Maine and the Maritime Provinces of Canada, and they like to bask in sunshine on rocks off Rome Point. They also appear at other places along the bay, but Rome Point may be the most reliable spot for seeing seals. The rocks off the point are close enough for walkers to watch the seals, through binoculars, but far enough away to avoid disturbing them.

This walk, about 2½ miles in and back, is relatively easy although it can be extremely cold in winter wind. So pick a day with both sunshine and calm air, and be sure to check the tide charts (available through newspapers and TV weather forecasts). The seals are most frequently seen at low tide, when more rocks are exposed, and in the two hours just before and just after low tide. As many as 170 seals have been counted at Rome Point at one time. My wife and I have seen 60 seals at low tide but also have been there at the wrong times and have had nos sightings or have noticed just a few heads bobbing in the swells. With seals, timing is everything.

The seals begin arriving in Narragansett Bay in October but the peak time for big numbers appears to be March. Some seals remain in the area until May.

While watching seals, or waiting for them to appear, winter visitors to Rome Point also can expect to see numerous birds on the water, including

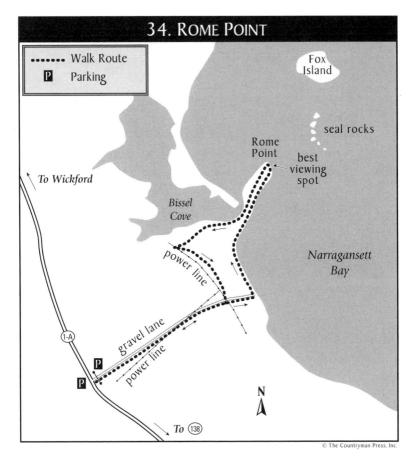

34. ROME POINT

© The Countryman Press, Inc.

loons, cormorants, gulls, and mergansers. In summer, terns frequently put on magnificent diving shows. On the way to the water, walkers usually can see many songbirds, winter or summer, in the brush that flanks the entrance lane.

My route includes returning part of the way back on trails that run among trees and bushes and is slightly longer than simply following the entrance lane and beach both ways. However, this longer route offers some different perspectives and perhaps chances of seeing more birds or even deer.

It is important not to disturb the seals at Rome Point.

Rome Point is owned by the state and has become increasingly popular in recent years. On a bright Saturday or Sunday afternoon you are likely to meet many walkers here, and it seems most are accompanied by dogs. A sign near the point close to the seal rocks says dogs must be leashed in that area to prevent them from frightening the seals. Any kind of harassment of the seals, whether intentional or otherwise, is punishable by a fine or even a jail term.

Access

From the north, take RI 1A through Wickford into the village of Hamilton. The entrance lane is 1.7 miles from a traffic light at Fairway Drive. From the south, the lane is just over 0.5 mile from RI 138. The gated lane runs to the east. Park along the highway.

Trail

You begin by following the straight, stony lane for about ½ mile. At first glance, the surrounding area is not particularly attractive, with small trees, abundant briars and brush, and a power line running along the right side. However, people who like birds will usually notice plenty of activity in the bushes. We've seen such "summer birds" as towhees, catbirds, robins, thrushes, and warblers here in December and January, along with such winter regulars as white-throated sparrows, kinglets, chickadees, and cardinals.

The power line crosses the lane just as the path makes its first curve, a slight bend to the right. Then, when the lane straightens again, you will reach another power line crossing overhead and will see paths crossing your lane. If walking the route described here, you will return on the path now on your left.

Continue on the entrance lane as it runs downhill toward to the bay, now within sight. The lane ends just before the beach, and for many walkers—those not primarily interested in seals—this is their destination. It is a rocky beach and not suitable for swimming, but it is a good place for children to explore. The shore is covered with millions of shells washed up from the bay.

To your right is the high Jamestown Bridge, and directly across the water is Conanicut Island, usually called Jamestown. Rome Point itself is to the left, and to get there you must walk the curving shoreline. Walking is usually easier up near the grass line rather than over the rocks and shells by the water.

As you walk, keep your eye on the water. Seals are curious animals and sometimes swim parallel to walkers. More often than not there are birds on or above the water.

If you have timed your walk to low tide, when you reach the point you will see a string of rocks in the water, just to the right of a small, one-house island called Fox Island. These rocks are the favorite haul-out spot for harbor seals, and they sometimes crowd together so tightly they appear to be resting on top of one another. They are visible with the naked eye but binoculars or a spotting scope help greatly in viewing these big (up to 4 feet long) creatures with dark eyes, flippers, and whiskers. At times there are so many seals some can't find room on the rocks and continue swimming nearby or occasionally leaping out of the water in a maneuver called "porpoising." That is probably the seals' most entertaining action.

When you're able to tear yourself away from the scene, you can simply retrace your steps. However, to begin your return walk, I recommend going into the trees on the point and finding a well-worn path that runs down the middle of this narrow peninsula. This path, which is welcome shelter from cold wind, follows the opposite side of the point from your earlier route. It passes beside thriving cedar trees and provides some excellent views of a small body of water called Bissel Cove, where you may see more birds or, in warm-weather months, clammers or kayakers.

This path continues circling to the right but stay on it only as far as a power line. Here, take a smaller trail to the left or follow the raised berm directly beneath the power line. The trail is more interesting. It weaves slightly through second-growth woods—I've seen deer here, and their antler rubs on trees—before taking you back to the entrance lane you walked earlier. At this junction, turn right and return uphill to your car.

35 · Ruecker Wildlife Refuge

Walking distance: 1½ miles
Walking time: 1 to 1½ hours

This walk is a little jewel. Looping through the Emilie Ruecker Wildlife Refuge, it is only 1½ miles long on an easy-to-walk path. If you like birds and fiddler crabs, you are likely to be fascinated nearly every step of the way.

You also are likely to see deer tracks on the trails and perhaps the deer themselves. Coyotes are common in this area, too, but are usually seen and heard only at night.

The refuge, located on the salty shores of the Sakonnet River in Tiverton, was a 30-acre farm before the owner, Emilie Ruecker, donated it to the Audubon Society of Rhode Island in 1965. Now, thanks to its natural attributes—shallow marshes, small fields, and upland woodlots—and Audubon management, the refuge attracts a wide variety of birdlife, particularly during the spring and fall migrations. The fiddler crabs and some unusual rock formations add to the attraction, but for most walkers it is the birds that make the trails of Ruecker so inviting.

Access

Follow RI 77 south from the village of Tiverton about 3 miles to Seapowet Road. Turn right and drive less than 0.5 mile to the refuge and parking lot, which are on the right.

Trail

As soon as you arrive, you will start hearing birds. In spring and early summer, you may hear quail and geese on the surrounding farms, and

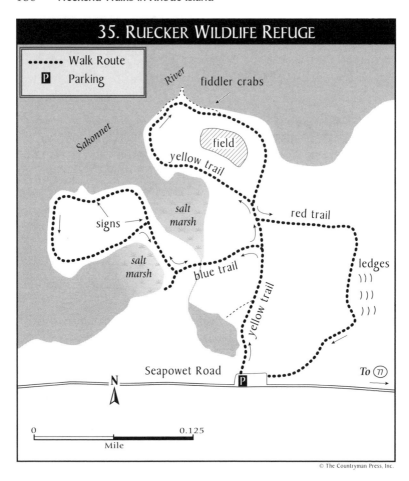

35. RUECKER WILDLIFE REFUGE

•••••• Walk Route
P Parking

River
fiddler crabs

Sakonnet

field

yellow trail

salt marsh

signs

red trail

salt marsh

blue trail

ledges

yellow trail

Seapowet Road

P

To 77

N

0   0.125
Mile

© The Countryman Press, Inc.

warblers and catbirds call from within the sanctuary's dense growth of bushes and small trees. In fall, migrating swallows, sometimes in the thousands, gather in this area before heading south. Over the course of a year, about 150 species of birds frequent this little refuge.

The main trails are named the Yellow, Blue, and Red Trails and are blazed accordingly. Several short side trails run to spots that provide views of the marshes. Even with frequent stops to observe the birds, you can easily walk all these trails in 1 to 1½ hours.

From the parking lot, take the Yellow Trail that starts beside a wooden kiosk, where trail maps are usually available. The trail runs through a small grove of cedars and hemlocks and you'll quickly come to a white-blazed path, going left, just before a stone wall. This path leads to a shallow pond. In most seasons, you can find herons, egrets, ducks, and perhaps bitterns, sandpipers, and other birds here.

Beyond the cedar grove, you enter the old farm fields, now overgrown with bushes, many of which produce berries that attract numerous birds. Several benches along the trails invite you to slow down and enjoy the bird activity. Catbirds are abundant here, along with mockingbirds, thrashers, orioles, thrushes, and goldfinches. In early spring, you may be able to see and hear the mating dance of woodcocks in the small fields kept open.

When you reach a sign for the Blue Trail loop, go left for a look at the salt marshes. The first segment takes you over a narrow brook, then onto a small peninsula. Short side trails lead to the shore for good views of the shallow water, which often draws herons, egrets, and swans. Tiny flowers called trailing arbutus can be found along the trail in spring, and dense shadbush and bayberry add color when in flower and later supply berries for birds such as cedar waxwings, cardinals, and titmice. A large sign along the trail indicates some species of larger birds that may be seen in the area.

When you complete the loop, return to the Yellow trail, and you soon reach a major trail junction. Pass the Red Trail on your right (you'll take it later) and, at a Y-intersection, take the left fork. This path, still part of the Yellow Trail, circles a larger peninsula, going all the way around an open field where birdhouses have been installed for bluebirds. This field is also where woodcocks put on their show in the April evenings. The Yellow Trail runs a few yards back from the shore for the most part, but several side paths enable you to go down to the sand, where you are likely to find fiddler crabs in summer. Hundreds of tiny holes in the sand betray their presence, and on warm, sunny days you may see hundreds of them scurrying across the beach or hiding just inside their burrows. For many

Salt marshes lie beside the Ruecker Refuge.

walkers, especially those with small children, the fiddlers may be the highlight of a visit to Ruecker.

After you finish the Yellow Trail loop, take the Red Trail, now going off to your left. Here, you enter the deepest woods on the refuge, although stone walls show that this area, too, once was farmland. Taller hardwoods are mixed with pines and cedars, and you will notice unusual boulders scattered about. These rocks appear to consist of small pebbles cemented together; local residents call the boulders puddingstone. This sedimentary bedrock, estimated to be 250 million years old, is found few other places than the Narragansett Bay basin.

The trail runs fairly near houses just off the refuge and winds along a low ridge of the puddingstone before curving right, back toward the refuge interior. It then runs through a dense, damp section equipped with wooden walkways and, too soon, emerges at the parking lot. But don't hurry off; sometimes the trees around the parking area offer another excellent variety of birds.

36 · Weetamoo Woods–
Pardon Gray Preserve

Walking distance: 5¼ miles
Walking time: 3 hours

Weetamoo Woods is owned by the town of Tiverton and the adjoining Pardon Gray Preserve is owned by the Tiverton Land Trust. Together, they encompass approximately 680 acres, and they offer much to walkers. Not only are there enough woodland delights and fields to satisfy those who enjoy nature, but the area is a history buff's bonanza.

The Weetamoo property is named for a female Indian sachem at the time of King Philip's War. Weetamoo is believed to have been married to Philip's brother and was considered a leader of the Pocasset tribe that spent its winters here. Pardon Gray was an officer in the Revolutionary War and is buried in a small family cemetery on the Land Trust property.

The route described here enables walkers to see the best of both properties. You will wander on ancient lanes through a thriving forest of oak, holly, beech, and hemlock, visit the remarkable stonework of a long-vanished sawmill, cross several stone bridges, climb an imposing outcropping for long views, look over open fields, visit the Gray cemetery, and walk for a while on a road named for the Marquis de Lafayette, who stayed in a nearby home briefly during the American Revolution.

Making the loop described here would mean a walk of about 5¼ miles. Those who want a shorter walk can easily trim the distance to about 2½ miles while still seeing the mill ruins, the outlook called High Rock, and a venerable landmark tree. The shorter route does not include the Gray cemetery or the open fields, but they can be examined with a short walk by entering the preserve from RI 77.

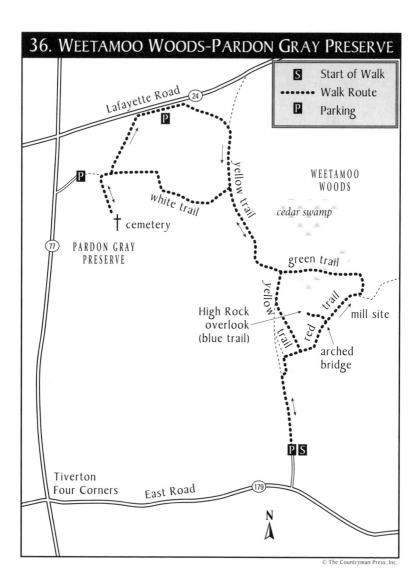

36. Weetamoo Woods-Pardon Gray Preserve

S Start of Walk
•••••• Walk Route
P Parking

Lafayette Road (24)

P

white trail

† cemetery

(77)

PARDON GRAY
PRESERVE

yellow trail

WEETAMOO
WOODS

cedar swamp

green trail

yellow trail

red trail

High Rock
overlook
(blue trail)

mill site

arched
bridge

P **S**

Tiverton
Four Corners   East Road   (179)

N

© The Countryman Press, Inc.

There are numerous side trails and paths, particularly in the early section, that can be confusing, so pay close attention to the blazes.

Access

Weetamoo Woods has several access points, but for this walk, drive to the south entrance, the most commonly used entrance. After entering Tiverton, follow RI 77 south just over 5 miles from the RI 24 junction to the crossroads village of Tiverton Four Corners. There, turn left onto East Road (RI 179) and drive just over ½ mile. Look for the Weetamoo Woods sign and a gravel lane on the left, just before a fire station on the opposite side of the road. The parking lot is about 150 yards down the lane.

Trail

The trail begins on what was Eight Rod Way, a road laid out in 1679 as the main north-south roadway on the original chartered township. The road through the swamp was settled, and several cellar holes remain, but this section of Eight Rod Way was eventually abandoned.

On this first segment, which is actually only a right-of-way to the Weetamoo property, you will cross the first two of many brooks. Most of the bridges are stone slabs laid in place many decades, and even centuries, ago. Stone walls flank the road in places. At about ⅓ mile, you reach a trail junction, the beginning of Weetamoo. Take a red-blazed trail that breaks off to the right of the main road.

This red path goes through an opening in a stone wall, then leads past a tumbled cellar hole, one of many on the property. Just beyond the cellar, the trail goes through a gap in another stone wall and turns right (the trail to the left goes off public property). Almost immediately you will pass two other trails, both on your left. The first is blazed in blue and the second in yellow. The yellow trail will be your return route. For now, however, stay with the red blazes, and ignore all side paths.

At about ½ mile from your start you will reach the unmistakable mill site. Huge cut stones lie just below a high stone and earth dam, and many are along a brook that runs from the dam and under a stone bridge on the

High Rock gets walkers above Weetamoo Woods.

red trail. The sawmill that stood here is believed to date to sometime in the 1800s, and a small portion of the millpond remains above the dam. Most impressive, though, is the bridge under your trail. Unlike the slab bridges, this one is built of stones wedged vertically, without mortar, into a low arch. Take a close look.

The red-blazed trail crosses the bridge and continues, but before going on you may want to follow a blue-blazed path that runs uphill, to the left, beside the mill. This short path will take you to High Rock, an outcropping that looms above the surrounding forest. The blue trail passes below the ledge but climb up and walk the outcropping's length to get full appreciation of its size. It is worth the effort, even though you will have to climb down where you went up.

Once down, return to the mill site and resume your walk on the red trail. Again, be sure you follow the blazes and don't wander off on other paths. About 100 yards beyond the mill, look for a narrow path blazed in green that breaks off to the left. The green trail is your connector through the interior of the forest and will take you to the yellow trail that is the main lane through Weetamoo.

The green trail's featured attraction is mountain laurel. There is so much laurel in this area that one section is called the Laurel Tunnel. Visit here in mid-June and you will be walking through a tunnel of white and pink flowers. But it is not all laurel. There also are stands of beech trees, more brooks, a wooden footbridge, and another stone bridge.

When you reach the yellow trail, you have gone about 1½ miles. A turn to the left would take you back to your car in another mile. Just ahead, however, on the yellow trail is one of the landmarks of the area, an immense oak tree estimated at 250 to 300 years old. Its outstretched limbs indicate it was growing when there were few other trees along this road.

Beyond the oak, the yellow trail weaves a bit but remains easy to travel, particularly since a walkway was built over a damp area. Stone walls are almost constantly in sight. You could walk this path all the way out to Lafayette Road, the northern boundary of Weetamoo, but those seeking a shorter walk but still interested in the Pardon Gray fields and the cemetery should keep an eye out for side trails off to the left. Take the *second* white-blazed path (the first goes out toward a recreation complex).

This second white trail goes through a stone wall, then curves to the left around a wetland and vernal pool. At this writing, this trail is not yet worn, so some care must be taken, but it is well marked. It wanders downhill through mixed forest that includes many holly trees, relatively rare elsewhere in Rhode Island, then suddenly emerges into an open field.

The Pardon Gray Preserve is about 230 acres and much of it continues to be farmed, usually in hay. Pardon Gray himself and members of his family are buried in a little stone-walled cemetery out in the field, marked by a clump of trees straight ahead as you leave the woods. However, in deference to the hay crop and the birds that nest in the tall grasses, visitors are asked not to walk directly to the cemetery. Instead, follow a farm lane along the edge of the woods to your right, and stay on the lane as it turns left. When you reach another lane going to the left, you can take that one to the graveyard, a most peaceful final resting place. Most of the tombstones are from the early 1800s.

From the cemetery, you can retrace your steps back across the field and up the white trail and turn right toward the yellow trail. However, if you want more walking, return on the farm lane you walked earlier, then take a grassy lane (see map) going to the north (left). It quickly leads to a white-blazed trail going left through dense woods. This trail ends at Lafayette Road. Turn right on the paved road and follow it past a parking lot for both Weetamoo and Pardon Gray, past a gate, and then a short distance more until seeing a side trail on the right. Take this trail.

Now you are again on the yellow trail and will follow it most of the way back through Weetamoo. This is a delightful segment with tall trees on both sides. For more than a mile you will follow this old road, eventually passing the two white trails you saw earlier, the old oak, the green trail, and the blue trail. When you reach the red trail, turn right and return up Eight Rod Way to your car.

37 · Simmons Mill Pond

Walking distance: 3 miles
Walking time: 2 to 2½ hours

Not many walkers know the Simmons Mill Pond Wildlife Management Area as yet, and those who have never been on its lanes are missing a delightful experience. Among the newer state properties, it offers miles of lanes and old roads, extensive woodlands, numerous ponds, and some open fields. Most of the lanes are flanked by stone walls and towering trees. Add it all up, and Simmons is an ideal place to walk in spring, when bird activity is highest, or in fall, when the foliage show is at its best.

The 445-acre property in Little Compton has been catering to wildlife for many years. Back when it was private property, its owners, particularly Bill Chace, created a wildlife haven by building a network of ponds in the forest. Now the ponds, connected by open lanes, attract ducks, geese, ospreys, herons, swallows, and numerous other birds, as well as such mammals as deer, mink, foxes, muskrats, and raccoons. The largest pond, the 18-acre millpond, is well known to area fishermen but walkers often have most of the property to themselves.

My wife and I have had some great wildlife experiences here, including a curious baby fox that kept popping out of its den to watch us and an irate mother grouse that attacked us when we apparently walked too near its nest or brood of chicks.

There are no blazed trails at Simmons, and many of the lanes run at confusing angles and some simply run off the property, so care must be taken when visiting for the first time. The route described here, which hits the best features and represents the easiest loop, is about 3 miles long. For

37. SIMMONS MILL POND

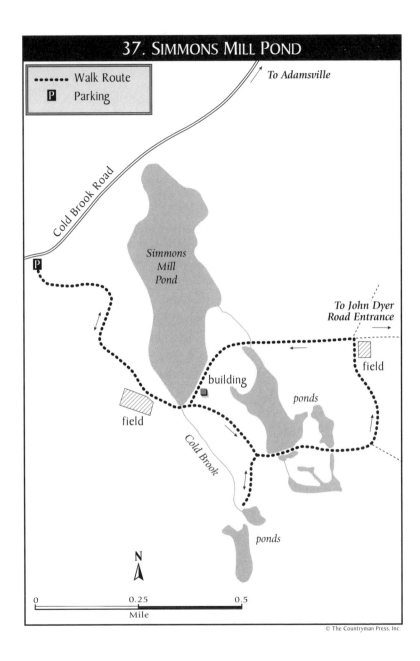

Walk Route

P Parking

To Adamsville

Cold Brook Road

Simmons
Mill
Pond

To John Dyer
Road Entrance

field

building

ponds

field

Cold Brook

ponds

N

0   0.25   0.5
Mile

© The Countryman Press, Inc.

those who want a longer walk, there are several other lanes that can be explored, although in most cases you'll have to turn back when you reach the boundaries of the state property.

As a state management area, Simmons is subject to hunting season regulations, including the wearing of orange from October to the end of February. Spring, however, is probably the best time to visit.

Access

Simmons has two entrances. For this walk, use the main parking lot on Cold Brook Road. Take RI 179 or RI 81 into Adamsville, then drive Cold Brook Road about 1.5 miles southwest to the entrance, on the left. A smaller parking lot is on John Dyer Road south of Adamsville.

Trail

For the first ½ mile, the trail is a gravel lane that runs through a mixed forest of mid-sized trees and dense underbrush. If you visit in spring, you are likely to find numerous birds as soon as you begin walking, most likely thrushes, towhees, warblers, catbirds, ovenbirds, and others. While the lane is barred to vehicle travel, it is easily wide enough for a car and walking is easy.

You'll pass a lane angling back to the right (one of several dead-end roads) and then see an open field on the right. This is one of the fields planted in grain each year for wildlife. You may see or hear pheasants or quail here and probably will find orioles or thrashers in the trees surrounding the field.

Just beyond the field, the lane runs across a dike that helped create the largest pond. To your left is 18-acre Simmons pond; chances are, you can see geese and ducks on the water and perhaps an osprey or two hovering above or perched in trees along the shore. This is also where you are likely to see fishermen. On the right side of the dike bridge, Cold Brook spills down through the woods.

Beyond the bridge, an inviting lane breaks off to the left, following the shore, and you can see a building at the water's edge. You could follow that lane now, but for this walk go straight ahead; you'll return on the lane by the building. It is a great place to rest after your walk.

The main entrance road, after leaving the large pond, is more grass than gravel. It curves to the right, passing beneath tall trees that provide shade in summer and colorful foliage in autumn. In ¼ mile, you reach another fork. If you wish, take the lane going to the right for a look at some of the smaller ponds, but then return to the intersection and resume walking the main road to the right. Shortly beyond the intersection, you reach a small bridge with a high dike on the left and several small ponds on the right. Go up on the dike for a good view of the second-largest pond on the property. Again, you are likely to see waterbirds of several varieties here. Paths to the right beside the bridge enable you to look over the smaller ponds.

After crossing another small bridge and more ponds, the road makes a long, sweeping curve to the left. Throughout this area, you'll find an interesting mixture of trees, including the relatively rare holly. Stone walls meander through the forest in some areas, and in some sections they flank the road. You'll soon see another road breaking off to the right, through an opening in a stone wall. That route is good for exploring—it leads to a brook, some wetland areas, and more wild forest—but it can be confusing, with several more branchings, and eventually runs off state land, so you'll have to return. For this walk, stay on the main road, turning left at the junction with the side road.

This next section is perhaps the most picturesque part of Simmons. Stone walls line the road and tall trees meet overhead. It was here where the female grouse rushed out and pecked at our boots. Most of the time, the birds are in the trees and the bushes. When you reach a small open field on your right, look to the left side of the road. You'll find a stone-lined well, capped with a large round stone, and a series of small stone-walled enclosures in the woods, possibly holding pens for livestock in another era.

Just beyond the field is still another crossroad. The main road runs straight ahead, beckoning with its tall trees and stone walls, but it quickly

Stone walls line some lanes at Simmons Mill Pond.

reaches the property boundary. The curvy lane to the right, the least worn of the four, goes to the John Dyer Road parking lot, a distance of about ⅓ mile. To continue this loop back to the millpond, turn to the left at the stone-walled intersection.

There are more side lanes leading off from this road; ignore them. In a few minutes, you reach a point where water may be crossing the road. Large stones on the left side are usually enough for you to cross without getting your feet wet. The pond on the left is the same one you saw earlier when you climbed the high dike at the series of ponds.

From this point, it is only a matter of minutes until you reach the building on the shore of Simmons Mill Pond. Once a retreat for the property owners, it was later used briefly as an education center. More recently it has been boarded up. However, a deck at the rear of the building remains a great place to linger a while and look over the pond. When ready to leave, and if you can tear yourself away, simply walk around the end of the pond to the bridge and retrace the ½ mile back to your car.

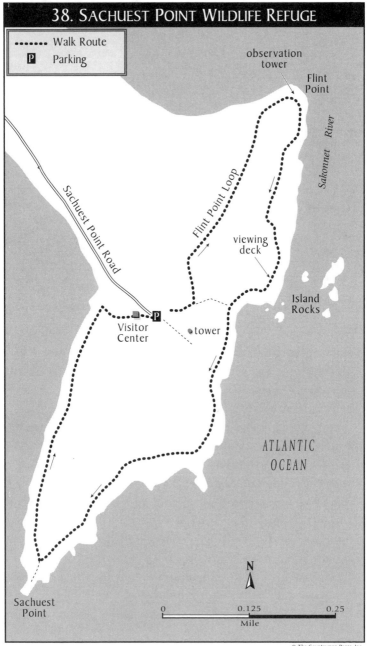

38. SACHUEST POINT WILDLIFE REFUGE

······ Walk Route
P Parking

observation
tower

Flint
Point

Sakonnet River

Flint Point Loop

viewing
deck

Island
Rocks

Visitor
Center

P

tower

ATLANTIC
OCEAN

Sachuest
Point Road

Sachuest
Point

N

0   0.125   0.25
Mile

© The Countryman Press, Inc.

38 · Sachuest Point Wildlife Refuge

Walking distance: 2½ miles
Walking time: 2 hours

This is a favorite spot for birders. Sachuest Point, a national wildlife refuge in Middletown, juts into Rhode Island Sound and apparently is on the migration route of a great many birds. As many as two hundred species have been identified here in a year.

A trail runs the perimeter of the 242-acre refuge, and there are observation platforms, including one with a telescope, and several benches to help visitors enjoy the views. The refuge also has a visitor center with restrooms and naturalists or volunteers are often on hand to answer questions. They also lead public nature events.

The walk described here is 2½ miles and follows the scenic shoreline. It is flat and easy and provides access to the rocky shore for those who want to try beachcombing. This route includes two of the raised observation platforms (the other is on an interior trail) and offers the best of Sachuest.

Fall and spring visits are suggested for two reasons. First, they are the migration seasons, when you are likely to see the most birds passing over the point or resting on the water. Also, in summer, the road leading to the refuge is often jammed with traffic because it is the only route to a nearby beach.

However, winter is becoming another popular time to visit Sachuest, despite its exposure to icy wind, because of the waterfowl that linger just offshore. Strikingly colorful harlequin ducks that appear at few other sites along the New England coast can often be found riding the turbulent waves around Sachuest. Short-eared owls and northern harriers hunt over the refuge fields in winter as well. And seals have been appearing more often in recent winters within view of walkers on the eastern side of Sachuest.

Access

Sachuest Point is at the extreme southeastern corner of Aquidneck Island. If you're coming across the Newport Bridge, follow RI 138 until it turns north (left) at the Middletown line, then go straight ahead on Miantonomi Avenue until after it becomes Green End Avenue. Continue on Green End until reaching Paradise Avenue, then turn south (right) and proceed until reaching Sachuest Point Road at the water. Follow signs to the left to the refuge.

If you're coming over the Mount Hope Bridge or from the Tiverton area, follow RI 138 south to Mitchells Lane, which is near the Portsmouth-Middletown line. Take Mitchells left to Green End Avenue, turn right for a short distance, then go left on Paradise Avenue to the beach. Sachuest Point is to the left.

Trail

Just behind the parking lot, to the left of the visitor center, is a kiosk, which makes a good starting point. A trail passes near the kiosk, and you can go two ways, but for this walk, go left. The other path goes into the interior of the refuge.

You are on the Flint Point Loop, and the trail quickly splits. I suggest going left at the junction and then following the perimeter of the refuge. You pass through a section filled with low bushes and vines, indicative of what was found through most of the refuge until recently, when much of the brush was removed and grasslands restored. Songbirds frequent the brush in spring and summer, and huge flocks of swallows sometimes gather here in fall. Owls and hawks may hunt in the open fields to the left.

In about ¼ mile, you reach the shore at Flint Point. The observation platform provides excellent views of a beach to your left and the wide Sakonnet River. Here you are likely to see your first waterbirds, perhaps

Looking for birds is part of most walks at Sachuest Point.

cormorants, mergansers, and swans as well as terns, gulls, and usually some sandpipers. In late fall and winter there may be flocks of lesser known waterfowl such as eiders, scoters, and perhaps the showy harlequin ducks.

The trail follows the shore but occasionally runs slightly inland, out of view of the water, for brief periods. Side paths lead down to the water. Farther offshore are huge rocks, where waves break in loud and picturesque fashion. We have seen seals on these rocks in winter. Across the river is the Little Compton shoreline and, far to your right, on a rock island, is the lighthouse of Sakonnet Point.

When you reach a trail junction, you've gone just over 1 mile. The path to the right runs back toward the visitor center. But continue following the shore. The views here are superb, with massive stone ledges where surf fishermen often gather. A viewing deck with a telescope helps you scan for waterfowl, many of which are depicted on a large sign.

After the trail curls to the right around a small cove, you begin seeing open fields on the right. Hawks and owls often hunt over these fields, too, and in winter you may see snowy owls, rare birds that spend the rest of the year in the Arctic. The new grasslands are likely to attract more nesting birds as time goes on.

The path takes you out to Sachuest Point itself, the southern tip of the refuge, and that is another good place to pause and watch the waves crash onto the mass of rocks. Here, you have water on three sides.

From the point, the trail curls around the western side of the refuge and heads back north. From this path, you can see Newport in the distance and the top of the Newport Bridge. You are also likely to see numerous sailboats during the warmer months.

The trail is higher above the water than on the east side of the refuge. As you proceed, you will see a beach area along the road you drove into the refuge. When you reach pavement, you are near the end. Turn right for the short walk to the visitor center.

39 · Cliff Walk

Walking distance: 6½ miles
Walking time: 3 to 3½ hours

Sooner or later, every Rhode Island walker, and many a visitor to the state, has to try Cliff Walk. It is the state's most famous trail, a 3½-mile walkway that follows part of the Newport shoreline, beginning at Easton's Beach. For the entire distance, you have the sea on one side and the magnificent mansions of another era on the other.

Development of Cliff Walk was begun in the 1880s and it was designated a National Historic Walking Trail in 1976.

In summer, this is a crowded walk, with numerous tourists using it not only for the ocean scenes but also to get a free look at the mansions, among the most lavish homes ever built in America. The trail runs behind dozens of these 60- and 70-room "cottages" built in the late 1800s when Newport was the playground of the Vanderbilts and Astors, the Whartons and Belmonts, and other leaders of industry and finance. Some of these mansions, which face Bellevue Avenue, are now open in warm-weather months as museumlike relics of a gilded age.

A sparkling spring or crisp autumn day might be best for this walk, because not only is the trail crowded in summer but also the heat tends to smudge the sea views. There is virtually no shade for the entire 3½ miles, and most of the walkway is concrete or stone, so a beating sun can make the hiking too hot.

If you walk the entire distance, you have to return, of course. For those who don't want to do Cliff Walk in both directions can walk back to Easton's Beach on city streets. In this way you can see the front of some of the mansions you passed behind as well as those on the opposite side of

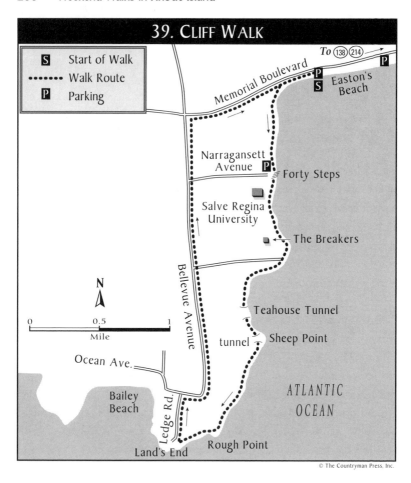

39. CLIFF WALK

S Start of Walk
••••••• Walk Route
P Parking

To (138) (214)

Memorial Boulevard

Easton's Beach

Narragansett Avenue

Forty Steps

Salve Regina University

The Breakers

Teahouse Tunnel

tunnel — Sheep Point

N

0   0.5   1
Mile

Bellevue Avenue

Ocean Ave.

Bailey Beach

Ledge Rd.

ATLANTIC OCEAN

Land's End   Rough Point

© The Countryman Press, Inc.

Bellevue Avenue. Returning to your start via Ledge Road, Bellevue Avenue, and Memorial Boulevard makes a walk of about 6½ miles—slightly shorter than a round-trip on Cliff Walk—and provides different perspectives, many immense shade trees, and several shops as well as the famed Tennis Casino and International Tennis Hall of Fame.

Be aware, if you are committed to walking the entire shoreline, that the final segment along the cliff is over large and potentially difficult rocks.

The trail also takes a pounding from the elements, including the crashing surf, and therefore suffers frequent damage.

Access

To reach Cliff Walk's start, take RI 138 into Newport, turn south on RI 138A or RI 214, and continue to Memorial Boulevard. Turn right and you will quickly reach the state-owned Easton's Beach, where you can park. Or you can take Memorial Boulevard east from the wharf area of downtown Newport. There is room for several cars on the street along the beach. Parking is free in off-season; meters are in operation in summer. The beach parking lot also carries a fee in summer but is free the rest of the year.

Many walkers also begin Cliff Walk by parking at the end of Narragansett Avenue, which runs off Bellevue. Beginning there means skipping the first segment of the trail but parking sometimes is easier and your walk would still include most of the route's highlights.

Trail

The trail's beginning, uphill from Easton's Beach, is well marked. You start behind a restaurant and quickly rise high above the sea. The path here is a sidewalk that twists and turns as it follows the shore. For the most part fences or hedges, or both, line the right side. On the left is the ocean. To the far left, across a cove, you can see Middletown, Easton Point, and Sachuest Point (Walk 38).

When you reach the first street (Narragansett Avenue) coming in from the right, you are at Forty Steps. Originally a natural rock formation that provided access to the water, it was a gathering place in Newport's Gilded Age for the servants who worked in the mansions. The steps have been replaced many times and now there is a concrete stairway with the steps bearing the names of benefactors. Above the stairway is an observation deck, which also serves as a memorial with several names inscribed in the stones. This is where many walkers begin and end their visit to Cliff Walk.

Beyond Forty Steps you can see many large buildings on the right; most of these are now part of Salve Regina University. Here you also encounter the first of many short stairways built into the trail. When you reach benches and a permanently open iron gate, you are behind The Breakers, the Italian-style palace Cornelius Vanderbilt commissioned in 1895. A rose hedge, a wrought-iron fence, and a vast lawn separate the trail from the mansion, but several breaks in the hedge enable you to marvel at the size of the 70-room "cottage."

After passing a second iron gate and several more immense homes, the trail runs behind a high white wall. On the other side of the wall is Rosecliff, the famed mansion used in filming the movie *The Great Gatsby*. Unfortunately, not much of Rosecliff can be seen from the trail.

Perhaps the most photographed feature on Cliff Walk looms a few hundred yards ahead. This is a Chinese-style teahouse, standing almost directly above the trail, that was used by Mrs. Otto Belmont for entertaining when she resided at Marble House. You pass almost under the pagoda through a curving tunnel. The trail then swings left and passes through another short tunnel in a rocky ridge called Sheep Point. Frequently, Cliff Walk visitors turn around at the teahouse or the tunnels and do not walk the final mile.

Beyond the tunnels, the path is gravel and dirt in some places but simply large rocks in other areas. Attempts were made to level the rocks but the footing can be hazardous, especially if the rocks are wet, so go slowly. At a small stairway, going down, you will see a sign imbedded in stone that warns: NEXT EXIT ⅞ MILE. PATH BECOMES ROCKY AND UNEVEN. IF YOU ARE UNSURE OF YOUR CAPABILITIES, TURN BACK NOW. However, if the rocks are dry and walkers are moderately agile, the final segment is not dangerous.

The route swings around the aptly named Rough Point, where surf often sprays high after crashing onto the boulders below. At times, the trail dips down low, passing just above the waves, and then climbs again. At one point you will find yourself beside a high chainlink fence with a relatively steep drop-off on the other side. In this area you cross a deep chasm on a wooden bridge, then there is another ¼ mile or so of rough footing before the path goes up and follows the edge of a fenced lawn. This area provides excellent views of several more huge homes.

A tunnel takes walkers under a Cliff Walk landmark.

When the trail breaks out onto a street, you will be facing the last mansion on the route, Land's End, once the George Eustis Paine estate. The street to your right is Ledge Road. Turn here if you plan to walk back on streets to Easton's Beach. When you reach the top of Ledge Road, turn right and take Bellevue all the way back to Memorial Boulevard, then take another right. The return is about 3 miles, most of it along what was once the most prestigious residential street in New England.

40 · Block Island

Walking distance: 9½ miles
Walking time: 4 to 4½ hours

I f you are looking for something different in your walking, take a trip to Block Island. There, you can walk for many miles and continue to see sights not available anywhere else in Rhode Island.

Block Island, 12 miles south of the mainland, was once a farming and fishing community. Later it was something of a resort and vacation spot, earning the nickname Bermuda of the North. The beaches and shops and restaurants still draw crowds in summer, but in autumn—the best time to visit the island—the place is a quieter wonderland of seascapes, cliffs, plant life, birds, and history.

The walk described here—9½ miles through the central and south-eastern regions of the island—is one of the most popular routes, although far more visitors use mopeds and bicycles than their feet. Except for a detour through a spot appropriately called the Greenway in the center of the island, and another through an intriguing place known as Rodman's Hollow, the distance is easily enough traveled on wheels, but I wonder if even mopeds and bikes are too fast; their riders may miss too much.

While October is a spectacular time on Block Island, be aware that the first weekend of October each year is when the Audubon Society of Rhode Island holds its Birding Weekend, to coincide with the peak of migrant bird activity, so the island is likely to be crowded at that time.

This long walk, much of it on pavement, can be very tiring. Go slowly, and enjoy the surroundings.

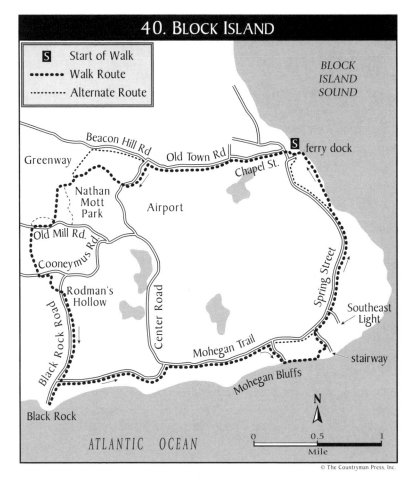

40. BLOCK ISLAND

S Start of Walk
•••••• Walk Route
········ Alternate Route

BLOCK
ISLAND
SOUND

Beacon Hill Rd

Greenway

Old Town Rd

Chapel St.

S ferry dock

Nathan
Mott
Park

Airport

Old Mill Rd.

Cooneymus Rd

Rodman's
Hollow

Center Road

Spring Street

Southeast
Light

Mohegan Trail

stairway

Black Rock Road

Mohegan Bluffs

Black Rock

N

ATLANTIC   OCEAN

0   0.5   1
Mile

© The Countryman Press, Inc.

Access

Unless you have your own boat, all Block Island visits begin and end at
the ferry landing in the village of New Shoreham at Old Harbor. The walk
can take 4 hours—or considerably longer if you linger at Mohegan Bluffs,
do extra exploring, or visit any of the shops—so it is best to take the
Point Judith ferry, which takes only an hour to reach the island. Taking
the earliest ferry will give you time to do this walk and catch a return
ferry the same day.

Ferry schedules change often, however, so check departure times in advance.

Trail

From the ferry dock, turn right onto the first street (Water Street) and then almost immediately go left onto Chapel Street, between the Harborside Inn and the New Shoreham House, two of the large wooden hotels built for tourists. Quickly, you leave the shops behind and start uphill into a residential area. Chapel Street soon merges with Old Town Road, and in minutes you reach the town hall and the island's interior.

If you are used to forest walks, you will note the absence of tall trees. Early settlers cut the trees in carving out their farms, and ocean winds that buffet the island, especially in winter, prevent new vegetation from gaining much height. Still, there is much greenery all around. Fruit trees line the first section of Old Town Road, and many are now being engulfed by swarming vines and bushes. In summer and early fall, wildflowers are common and colorful.

When you reach Center Road, about 1 mile from your start and marked by millstones set in the ground, turn left and begin climbing a hill. In this area you'll pass the first entrance, on the right, into the Greenway, but do not enter just yet. That trail would take you north, and you want to go south. You also could visit the Greenway by going up Beacon Hill Road, on your right, to another entrance. However, if you want to go all the way to Mohegan Bluffs on your walk, you will not want to spend all day in the Greenway.

Instead, follow signs for the island airport and enter the Greenway on the opposite side of Center Road at a place called the Nathan Mott Park. By now, you might want a respite from pavement walking and the Greenway is perfect for that, offering grassy, walkers-only paths that weave through an extensive area permanently saved from development. This is a segment of Block Island the casual tourist rarely sees: many acres of dense vegetation, numerous songbirds and flowers, and excellent chances of seeing deer, butterflies, and perhaps some of the resident pheasants.

It is tempting to spend hours exploring the Greenway, but to leave time for completing your walk, take the entrance path up a high stairway and turn left, following signs toward the Turnip Farm. At the top of these stairs, however, linger for a moment. This area was recently cleared and now provides sweeping views of the airport and other parts of the island, including some of the stone walls left from the farming days.

In this cleared area is a sign indicating a path to Old Mill Road, and you will have to cross that road, but instead of taking that path stay on the trail into Turnip Farm. There is nothing left of the turnip patches but this trail is a better route out to Old Mill Road, passing through attractive overgrown fields with numerous side paths. By turning left at each junction, you'll soon be going downhill behind a house (on your left) toward a gate that indicates Old Mill Road. Just before reaching that gate, though, take note of a high fence on the right. It appears to be an animal pen but is actually a means of keeping deer from eating the northern blazing star, an endangered wildflower.

Just beyond this high fence, a path breaks to the right, and you could take it, with more left turns, out to Old Mill Road, but it is simpler to go through the gate out to the gravel road and turn right. In about ¼ mile, you reach the spot where you can return to the trail, now on your left. A ladder over a stone wall takes you back into brush for the short walk down to Cooneymus Road and Rodman's Hollow.

At Cooneymus Road, the trail plunges directly back into a thicket but then quickly curves left to a wonderful old dirt road, Black Rock Road, which skirts the edge of Rodman's Hollow, one of the island's natural highlights. The deep hollow is the favorite haunt of the Block Island meadow vole, a mouselike animal found nowhere else on earth. Hawks that feed on the vole and other small prey frequently soar over the hollow, and many songbirds gather here, particularly in migration season.

There are several paths that lead into the hollow, and exploring can be fun, but it also can be confusing. I suggest only short ventures and then return to Black Rock Road. This old road (no mopeds allowed) is a gem in itself and is one of my favorite walking places on the entire island. It

Southeast Light may be the most famous feature on Block Island.

runs about 1 mile to the south shore, and from this rutted lane you can often see deer or, at the very least, deer tracks. You'll also have long views, to the right, of meadows and rolling hills sectioned off by stone walls.

When you begin seeing the ocean straight ahead, look on your left for another dirt road; it will be your route toward Mohegan Bluffs. However, for now, stay on Black Rock Road to its end atop a high cliff overlooking the Atlantic Ocean. This is roughly the halfway point in your walk and is a great place to linger. You can take a path down to the stony beach, but be careful; the cliffs are fragile and a fatal accident occurred here in 2003 when a section fell onto a boy.

To resume, return to the side road you passed earlier and take it, now to the right. This road is fairly long and passes several homes, plus some impressive overlooks, before reaching pavement. Turn right onto the paved road, Mohegan Trail, toward the island's most famous cliffs.

The bluffs were named for the Mohegan war party that was driven over these cliffs by the island's residents, the Manisseans, in 1590. The highest bluffs tower 200 feet above the ocean, and you can reach the bluffs by two chief cutoffs.

I like to take the first side trail, an unmarked sandy path that runs through low brush from a point where the paved road jogs left. The path ends at a cliff that provides spectacular views of bluffs on both sides as well as a look at the Southeast Lighthouse in the distance to the left.

From this point, the agile can take a rather steep path to the right down to the beach, then walk the beach a few hundred yards to the left, and climb back up via a long stairway. However, if the climb down this cliff does not appeal to you, simply return to the paved road and go right to the next dirt lane at a sign for the Payne Overlook. At this writing, the popular overlook platform is gone—it was destroyed in a storm—but the 160-step stairway remains and enables you to reach the beach if so desired. For many island visitors, a climb down these stairs and back up is the ultimate accomplishment.

Back on the paved road, turn right and you'll quickly reach Southeast Light, an often-photographed lighthouse that was moved 245 feet in 1993 because of fears that it, too, would eventually be a victim of the eroding cliffs. The lighthouse beam carries 30 miles out to sea, and a strong light is necessary. As an engraved stone near the lighthouse indicates, many ships have gone down just off the island. At times, the lighthouse grounds are open to visitors and a museum is being developed.

Beyond the lighthouse, the road turns back toward the village and becomes Spring Street. In summer, you are likely to be dodging mopeds and bicycles in this segment but in other seasons it can be an easy, mostly downhill walk.

When the road runs near the water you may want to leave the pavement one last time. Cross the guardrail and take a path down to aptly named Pebbly Beach. It's just a short walk on this beach to a restaurant, an excellent place to refresh yourself while awaiting your ferry back to the mainland.

Index